ONE PROVERB EACH DAY

3 - YEAR JOURNAL

This Journal Belongs To:

_____

_____

_____

_____

The story behind this journal:

For as long as I can remember, I've always loved the idea of journaling—recording my day-to-day activities and reflecting on them from time-to-time, especially at yearend. To take the time to reflect on the things that I had done, the emotions I felt, the people and moments that impacted my life both positively and negatively, the things that I had yet to do to change my narrative, etc.

I've collected a stack of journals over the years that are currently tucked away in piles in various nooks and crannies all over my house. All kinds of journals—blank page journals, daily entry journals, fill-in-the-blank ones, insert the date of the entry journals, writing prompts ones, etc. The colors vary too. Black, brown, floral, brightly colored patterns, animal prints and more.

To be honest, journals were mostly unfinished until 2013 when I stumbled across a 5-year one-sentence journal. I had never seen anything like it. It seemed simple and easy to do—one sentence a day. I remember saying to myself, "If I can't do this, then my dreams of journaling every day is definitely doomed." I also thought that the reward to stick with it all year long would be to compare my entries to the day, each year, which was a big motivation for me. I made the purchase and amazingly stuck with it all year long and beyond.

Today I make an entry each night before I lay down to sleep. I've learned a lot about myself and how I respond to people and things that happen in my life from day to day. I also see patterns of things that I am not necessarily proud of and I make a plan to change my actions or responses. I've been reminded so many times that I am blessed and that I have so much to live for and to give to my family, friends and world. Journaling keeps me humble, proud, grateful, driven, hopeful and more. My 5-year one-sentence journal can finally join the stacks of journal books. However, this time it will be finished with no gaps of blank pages. Only memories and parts of my life's story collected over the years, resulting in over one thousand and eight hundred entries!

Once I finished my 5-year journal, I decided that I would like a 3-year one with room for 3-5 sentences. I began my search to find such a journal but had no luck, so I decided to create one---and here we are.

Long story short, I married my love for journaling and my love for African proverbs in a 3-year brief entry journal. This journal includes inspirational African proverbs to feed the soul and impart wisdom throughout the year.

I hope you will enjoy and benefit from the combination of things that I love—reflection, redemption, and wisdom. May you record memories and discoveries that will be treasured for years to come-- over one thousand entries to treasure!

Happy journaling!

Rita

1 JANUARY

He who is covered with other people's clothes is naked. – African proverb

Yr_____

_____
_____
_____
_____
_____
_____
_____

Yr_____

_____
_____
_____
_____
_____
_____
_____

Yr_____

_____
_____
_____
_____
_____
_____
_____

2 JANUARY

A bird that flies off the earth and lands on an anthill is still on the ground. — African proverb

Yr_____

_____

_____

_____

_____

_____

_____

_____

Yr_____

_____

_____

_____

_____

_____

_____

Yr_____

_____

_____

_____

_____

_____

_____

_____

3 JANUARY

You must attend to your business with the vendor in the market, and not to the noise of the market. — African proverb

Yr_____

_____
_____
_____
_____
_____
_____
_____
_____

Yr_____

_____
_____
_____
_____
_____
_____
_____
_____

Yr_____

_____
_____
_____
_____
_____
_____
_____
_____

4 JANUARY

He who is unable to dance says that the yard is stony. — African proverb

Yr_____

_____
_____
_____
_____
_____
_____
_____

Yr_____

_____
_____
_____
_____
_____
_____

Yr_____

_____
_____
_____
_____
_____
_____
_____

5 JANUARY

You cannot name a child that is not born. — African proverb

Yr_____

_____
_____
_____
_____
_____
_____
_____

Yr_____

_____
_____
_____
_____
_____
_____
_____

Yr_____

_____
_____
_____
_____
_____
_____
_____

6 JANUARY

When you show the moon to a child, it sees only your finger. — African proverb

Yr_____

_____
_____
_____
_____
_____
_____
_____

Yr_____

_____
_____
_____
_____
_____
_____
_____

Yr_____

_____
_____
_____
_____
_____
_____
_____

7 JANUARY

Even as the archer loves the arrow that flies, so too he loves the bow
that remains constant in his hands. — African proverb

Yr_____

_____
_____
_____
_____
_____
_____
_____

Yr_____

_____
_____
_____
_____
_____
_____
_____

Yr_____

_____
_____
_____
_____
_____
_____
_____
_____

8 JANUARY

Knowledge without wisdom is like water in the sand. – African proverb

Yr_____

_____
_____
_____
_____
_____
_____
_____
_____

Yr_____

_____
_____
_____
_____
_____
_____
_____
_____

Yr_____

_____
_____
_____
_____
_____
_____
_____
_____
_____

9 JANUARY

To get lost is to learn the way. – African Proverb

Yr_____

_____
_____
_____
_____
_____
_____
_____
_____

Yr_____

_____
_____
_____
_____
_____
_____
_____
_____

Yr_____

_____
_____
_____
_____
_____
_____
_____
_____
_____

10 JANUARY

You learn how to cut down trees by cutting them down. – African proverb

Yr_____

_____

_____

_____

_____

_____

_____

_____

Yr_____

_____

_____

_____

_____

_____

_____

_____

Yr_____

_____

_____

_____

_____

_____

_____

_____

11 JANUARY

When you follow in the path of your father, you learn to walk like him. –
African proverb

Yr_____

_____
_____
_____
_____
_____
_____
_____

Yr_____

_____
_____
_____
_____
_____
_____
_____

Yr_____

_____
_____
_____
_____
_____
_____
_____

12 JANUARY

A fight between grasshoppers is a joy to the crow. – African proverb

Yr_____

_____
_____
_____
_____
_____
_____
_____
_____

Yr_____

_____
_____
_____
_____
_____
_____
_____

Yr_____

_____
_____
_____
_____
_____
_____
_____
_____

13 JANUARY

Unity is strength, division is weakness. — African proverb

Yr_____

_____
_____
_____
_____
_____
_____
_____
_____

Yr_____

_____
_____
_____
_____
_____
_____
_____
_____

Yr_____

_____
_____
_____
_____
_____
_____
_____
_____

14 JANUARY

A family tie is like a tree, it can bend but it cannot break. – African proverb

Yr_____

_____

_____

_____

_____

_____

_____

_____

Yr_____

_____

_____

_____

_____

_____

_____

_____

Yr_____

_____

_____

_____

_____

_____

_____

_____

15 JANUARY

One cannot both feast and become rich. — African proverb

Yr_____

_____
_____
_____
_____
_____
_____
_____
_____

Yr_____

_____
_____
_____
_____
_____
_____
_____

Yr_____

_____
_____
_____
_____
_____
_____
_____
_____

16 JANUARY

What you give you get, ten times over. – African proverb

Yr_____

_____
_____
_____
_____
_____
_____
_____

Yr_____

_____
_____
_____
_____
_____
_____
_____

Yr_____

_____
_____
_____
_____
_____
_____
_____

17 JANUARY

You must judge a man by the work of his hands. – African proverb

Yr_____

_____
_____
_____
_____
_____
_____
_____

Yr_____

_____
_____
_____
_____
_____
_____
_____

Yr_____

_____
_____
_____
_____
_____
_____
_____

18 JANUARY

You have little power over what's not yours. — African proverb

Yr_____

_____

_____

_____

_____

_____

_____

_____

Yr_____

_____

_____

_____

_____

_____

_____

_____

Yr_____

_____

_____

_____

_____

_____

_____

_____

_____

19 JANUARY

The mouth which eats does not talk. – African proverb

Yr_____

_____
_____
_____
_____
_____
_____
_____
_____

Yr_____

_____
_____
_____
_____
_____
_____
_____

Yr_____

_____
_____
_____
_____
_____
_____
_____
_____

20 JANUARY

Do not look where you fell, but where you slipped. — African proverb

Yr_____

_____

_____

_____

_____

_____

_____

_____

Yr_____

_____

_____

_____

_____

_____

_____

Yr_____

_____

_____

_____

_____

_____

_____

_____

21 JANUARY

Only a fool tests the depth of the river with both feet. — *African proverb*

Yr_____

_____

_____

_____

_____

_____

_____

_____

_____

Yr_____

_____

_____

_____

_____

_____

_____

_____

Yr_____

_____

_____

_____

_____

_____

_____

_____

_____

22 JANUARY

Water is colorless and tasteless but you can live on it longer than eating food. – African proverb

Yr_____

_____

_____

_____

_____

_____

_____

_____

Yr_____

_____

_____

_____

_____

_____

_____

_____

Yr_____

_____

_____

_____

_____

_____

_____

_____

23 JANUARY

Don't set sail on someone else's star. — African proverb

Yr_____

_____

_____

_____

_____

_____

_____

_____

Yr_____

_____

_____

_____

_____

_____

_____

Yr_____

_____

_____

_____

_____

_____

_____

_____

24 JANUARY

Patience attracts happiness; it brings near that which is far. — African proverb

Yr_____

_____
_____
_____
_____
_____
_____
_____

Yr_____

_____
_____
_____
_____
_____
_____
_____

Yr_____

_____
_____
_____
_____
_____
_____
_____

25 JANUARY

Marriage is like a groundnut; you have to crack it to see what is inside. –
African proverb

Yr_____

_____

_____

_____

_____

_____

_____

Yr_____

_____

_____

_____

_____

_____

_____

Yr_____

_____

_____

_____

_____

_____

_____

26 JANUARY

Where there is love there is no darkness. — African proverb

Yr_____

_____
_____
_____
_____
_____
_____
_____
_____

Yr_____

_____
_____
_____
_____
_____
_____
_____

Yr_____

_____
_____
_____
_____
_____
_____
_____
_____

27 JANUARY

Beautiful words don't put porridge in the pot. — African proverb

Yr_____

_____

_____

_____

_____

_____

_____

_____

_____

Yr_____

_____

_____

_____

_____

_____

_____

_____

_____

Yr_____

_____

_____

_____

_____

_____

_____

_____

_____

28 JANUARY

If there is character, ugliness becomes beauty; if there is none, beauty becomes ugliness. — African proverb

Yr_____

_____
_____
_____
_____
_____
_____
_____

Yr_____

_____
_____
_____
_____
_____
_____

Yr_____

_____
_____
_____
_____
_____
_____
_____

29 JANUARY

Return to old watering holes for more than water; friends and dreams are there to meet you. — African proverb

Yr_____

_____
_____
_____
_____
_____
_____
_____
_____

Yr_____

_____
_____
_____
_____
_____
_____
_____

Yr_____

_____
_____
_____
_____
_____
_____
_____
_____

30 JANUARY

Dine with a stranger but save your love for your family. — African proverb

Yr_____

_____
_____
_____
_____
_____
_____
_____
_____

Yr_____

_____
_____
_____
_____
_____
_____
_____

Yr_____

_____
_____
_____
_____
_____
_____
_____
_____

31 JANUARY

He who thinks he is leading and has no one following him is only taking a walk. — African proverb

Yr_____

_____
_____
_____
_____
_____
_____
_____

Yr_____

_____
_____
_____
_____
_____
_____
_____

Yr_____

_____
_____
_____
_____
_____
_____
_____
_____

1 FEBRUARY

He that beats the drum for the mad man to dance is no better than the mad man himself. — African proverb

Yr_____

_____

_____

_____

_____

_____

_____

_____

Yr_____

_____

_____

_____

_____

_____

_____

_____

Yr_____

_____

_____

_____

_____

_____

_____

_____

2 FEBRUARY

If you are building a house and a nail breaks, do you stop building or do you change the nail? — African proverb

Yr_____

_____
_____
_____
_____
_____
_____
_____
_____

Yr_____

_____
_____
_____
_____
_____
_____
_____

Yr_____

_____
_____
_____
_____
_____
_____
_____
_____

3 FEBRUARY

Anger and madness are brothers. — African proverb

Yr_____

_____
_____
_____
_____
_____
_____
_____
_____
_____

Yr_____

_____
_____
_____
_____
_____
_____
_____
_____
_____

Yr_____

_____
_____
_____
_____
_____
_____
_____
_____
_____

4 FEBRUARY

A flea can trouble a lion more than a lion can trouble a flea. — African proverb

Yr_____

_____
_____
_____
_____
_____
_____
_____

Yr_____

_____
_____
_____
_____
_____
_____
_____

Yr_____

_____
_____
_____
_____
_____
_____
_____

5 FEBRUARY

If you want to go fast, go alone. If you want to go far, go together. —
African proverb

Yr_____

_____
_____
_____
_____
_____
_____
_____
_____

Yr_____

_____
_____
_____
_____
_____
_____
_____

Yr_____

_____
_____
_____
_____
_____
_____
_____
_____

6 FEBRUARY

When an old man dies, a library burns to the ground with him. — African proverb

Yr_____

_____

_____

_____

_____

_____

_____

_____

Yr_____

_____

_____

_____

_____

_____

_____

_____

Yr_____

_____

_____

_____

_____

_____

_____

_____

7 FEBRUARY

However long the night, the dawn will always break. — African proverb

Yr_____

_____
_____
_____
_____
_____
_____
_____

Yr_____

_____
_____
_____
_____
_____
_____

Yr_____

_____
_____
_____
_____
_____
_____
_____

8 FEBRUARY

An army of sheep led by a lion can defeat an army of lions led by a sheep. – African proverb

Yr_____

_____

_____

_____

_____

_____

_____

_____

Yr_____

_____

_____

_____

_____

_____

_____

_____

Yr_____

_____

_____

_____

_____

_____

_____

_____

9 FEBRUARY

One who causes others misfortune also teaches them wisdom. – African Proverb

Yr_____

_____
_____
_____
_____
_____
_____
_____

Yr_____

_____
_____
_____
_____
_____
_____
_____

Yr_____

_____
_____
_____
_____
_____
_____
_____

10 FEBRUARY

When you befriend a chief remember that he sits on a rope. – African proverb

Yr_____

_____

_____

_____

_____

_____

_____

_____

_____

Yr_____

_____

_____

_____

_____

_____

_____

_____

Yr_____

_____

_____

_____

_____

_____

_____

_____

_____

11 FEBRUARY

It takes a whole village to raise a child. – African Proverb

Yr_____

_____
_____
_____
_____
_____
_____
_____

Yr_____

_____
_____
_____
_____
_____
_____
_____

Yr_____

_____
_____
_____
_____
_____
_____
_____
_____

12 FEBRUARY

Do not call the forest that shelters you a jungle. — African proverb

Yr_____

_____

_____

_____

_____

_____

_____

_____

Yr_____

_____

_____

_____

_____

_____

_____

Yr_____

_____

_____

_____

_____

_____

_____

_____

13 FEBRUARY

Ashes fly back into the face of him who throws them. — African Proverb

Yr_____

_____
_____
_____
_____
_____
_____
_____

Yr_____

_____
_____
_____
_____
_____
_____
_____

Yr_____

_____
_____
_____
_____
_____
_____
_____
_____

14 FEBRUARY

One must talk little and listen much. — African Proverb

Yr_____

_____
_____
_____
_____
_____
_____
_____
_____

Yr_____

_____
_____
_____
_____
_____
_____
_____

Yr_____

_____
_____
_____
_____
_____
_____
_____
_____

15 FEBRUARY

A family is like a forest, when you are outside it is dense, when you are inside you see that each tree has its place. – African Proverb

Yr_____

_____
_____
_____
_____
_____
_____
_____

Yr_____

_____
_____
_____
_____
_____
_____

Yr_____

_____
_____
_____
_____
_____
_____

16 FEBRUARY

If you're not part of the solution, you're part of the problem. – African Proverb

Yr_____

_____
_____
_____
_____
_____
_____
_____

Yr_____

_____
_____
_____
_____
_____
_____
_____

Yr_____

_____
_____
_____
_____
_____
_____
_____
_____

17 FEBRUARY

When a needle falls into a deep well, many people will look into the well, but few will be ready to go down after it. – African Proverb

Yr_____

_____
_____
_____
_____
_____
_____
_____

Yr_____

_____
_____
_____
_____
_____
_____
_____

Yr_____

_____
_____
_____
_____
_____
_____
_____
_____

18 FEBRUARY

The food eaten first lasts longest in the stomach. — African proverb

Yr_____

_____

_____

_____

_____

_____

_____

_____

Yr_____

_____

_____

_____

_____

_____

_____

Yr_____

_____

_____

_____

_____

_____

_____

_____

19 FEBRUARY

If you are looking for a fly in your food it means that you are full. —
African Proverb

Yr_____

_____
_____
_____
_____
_____
_____
_____
_____

Yr_____

_____
_____
_____
_____
_____
_____
_____
_____

Yr_____

_____
_____
_____
_____
_____
_____
_____
_____

20 FEBRUARY

No one gets a mouthful of food by picking between another person's teeth. – African Proverb

Yr_____

_____
_____
_____
_____
_____
_____
_____
_____

Yr_____

_____
_____
_____
_____
_____
_____
_____
_____

Yr_____

_____
_____
_____
_____
_____
_____
_____
_____

21 FEBRUARY

One who eats alone cannot discuss the taste of the food with others. —
African Proverb

Yr_____

_____

_____

_____

_____

_____

_____

_____

_____

Yr_____

_____

_____

_____

_____

_____

_____

_____

Yr_____

_____

_____

_____

_____

_____

_____

_____

_____

22 FEBRUARY

Don't take another mouthful before you have swallowed what is in your mouth. – African Proverb

Yr_____

_____
_____
_____
_____
_____
_____
_____

Yr_____

_____
_____
_____
_____
_____
_____
_____

Yr_____

_____
_____
_____
_____
_____
_____
_____
_____

23 FEBRUARY

To love the king is not bad, but a king who loves you is better. — African Proverb

Yr_____

_____
_____
_____
_____
_____
_____
_____
_____

Yr_____

_____
_____
_____
_____
_____
_____
_____

Yr_____

_____
_____
_____
_____
_____
_____
_____
_____
_____

24 FEBRUARY

Despite the beauty of the moon, sun and the stars, the sky also has a threatening thunder and striking lightening. – African Proverb

Yr_____

_____
_____
_____
_____
_____
_____
_____

Yr_____

_____
_____
_____
_____
_____
_____
_____

Yr_____

_____
_____
_____
_____
_____
_____
_____
_____

25 FEBRUARY

There is no beauty but the beauty of action. — African Proverb

Yr_____

_____
_____
_____
_____
_____
_____
_____
_____

Yr_____

_____
_____
_____
_____
_____
_____
_____

Yr_____

_____
_____
_____
_____
_____
_____
_____
_____

26 FEBRUARY

If ten cents does not go out, it does not bring in one thousand dollars. –
African Proverb

Yr_____

_____

_____

_____

_____

_____

_____

_____

Yr_____

_____

_____

_____

_____

_____

_____

_____

Yr_____

_____

_____

_____

_____

_____

_____

_____

27 FEBRUARY

If your cornfield is far from your house, the birds will eat your corn. —
African Proverb

Yr_____

_____
_____
_____
_____
_____
_____
_____

Yr_____

_____
_____
_____
_____
_____
_____
_____

Yr_____

_____
_____
_____
_____
_____
_____
_____

28 FEBRUARY

The wealth which enslaves the owner isn't wealth. – African Proverb

Yr_____

_____
_____
_____
_____
_____
_____
_____
_____

Yr_____

_____
_____
_____
_____
_____
_____
_____
_____

Yr_____

_____
_____
_____
_____
_____
_____
_____
_____

29 FEBRUARY

Make some money but don't let money make you. — African Proverb

Yr_____

_____
_____
_____
_____
_____
_____
_____

Yr_____

_____
_____
_____
_____
_____
_____
_____

Yr_____

_____
_____
_____
_____
_____
_____
_____
_____

1 MARCH

Where water is the boss there the land must obey. — African proverb

Yr_____

_____
_____
_____
_____
_____
_____
_____
_____

Yr_____

_____
_____
_____
_____
_____
_____
_____

Yr_____

_____
_____
_____
_____
_____
_____
_____
_____

2 MARCH

No matter how beautiful and well-crafted a coffin might look, it will not make anyone wish for death. — African proverb

Yr_____

_____
_____
_____
_____
_____
_____
_____

Yr_____

_____
_____
_____
_____
_____
_____
_____

Yr_____

_____
_____
_____
_____
_____
_____
_____

3 MARCH

The stone that is under water never knows when it rains. - African proverb

Yr_____

_____

_____

_____

_____

_____

_____

_____

Yr_____

_____

_____

_____

_____

_____

_____

_____

Yr_____

_____

_____

_____

_____

_____

_____

_____

4 MARCH

Do not expect to be offered a chair when you are visiting a place where the chief sits on the floor. - African Proverb

Yr_____

_____

_____

_____

_____

_____

_____

_____

Yr_____

_____

_____

_____

_____

_____

_____

_____

Yr_____

_____

_____

_____

_____

_____

_____

_____

_____

5 MARCH

You never miss the well until the water runs dry. – African Proverb

Yr_____

_____
_____
_____
_____
_____
_____
_____
_____

Yr_____

_____
_____
_____
_____
_____
_____
_____

Yr_____

_____
_____
_____
_____
_____
_____
_____
_____

6 MARCH

An old person is always uneasy when dry bones are mentioned in a proverb.— African proverb

Yr_____

_____
_____
_____
_____
_____
_____
_____

Yr_____

_____
_____
_____
_____
_____
_____
_____

Yr_____

_____
_____
_____
_____
_____
_____
_____
_____

7 MARCH

Between true friends even water drunk together is sweet enough. —
African proverb

Yr_____

_____
_____
_____
_____
_____
_____
_____

Yr_____

_____
_____
_____
_____
_____
_____
_____

Yr_____

_____
_____
_____
_____
_____
_____
_____
_____

8 MARCH

A stream cannot rise above its source. – African proverb

Yr_____

_____

_____

_____

_____

_____

_____

_____

_____

Yr_____

_____

_____

_____

_____

_____

_____

_____

Yr_____

_____

_____

_____

_____

_____

_____

_____

_____

9 MARCH

A cutting word is worse than a bowstring, a cut May heal, but the cut of the tongue does not. – African Proverb

Yr_____

_____
_____
_____
_____
_____
_____
_____
_____

Yr_____

_____
_____
_____
_____
_____
_____
_____

Yr_____

_____
_____
_____
_____
_____
_____
_____
_____

10 MARCH

The food that is in the mouth is not yet in the belly. — African proverb

Yr_____

_____
_____
_____
_____
_____
_____
_____

Yr_____

_____
_____
_____
_____
_____
_____
_____

Yr_____

_____
_____
_____
_____
_____
_____
_____
_____

11 MARCH

There are many colorful flowers on the path of life, but the prettiest have the sharpest thorns. – African proverb

Yr_____

_____
_____
_____
_____
_____
_____
_____

Yr_____

_____
_____
_____
_____
_____
_____
_____

Yr_____

_____
_____
_____
_____
_____
_____
_____
_____

12 MARCH

Do not let what you cannot do tear from your hands what you can. –
African proverb

Yr_____

_____

_____

_____

_____

_____

_____

_____

Yr_____

_____

_____

_____

_____

_____

_____

Yr_____

_____

_____

_____

_____

_____

_____

_____

13 MARCH

Wisdom is not like money to be tied up and hidden. – African proverb

Yr_____

_____

_____

_____

_____

_____

_____

_____

Yr_____

_____

_____

_____

_____

_____

_____

_____

Yr_____

_____

_____

_____

_____

_____

_____

_____

_____

14 MARCH

When brothers fight to the death, a stranger inherits their father's estate. — African proverb

Yr_____

_____

_____

_____

_____

_____

_____

_____

Yr_____

_____

_____

_____

_____

_____

_____

_____

Yr_____

_____

_____

_____

_____

_____

_____

_____

15 MARCH

Two ants do not fail to pull one grasshopper. — African proverb

Yr_____

_____

_____

_____

_____

_____

_____

_____

_____

Yr_____

_____

_____

_____

_____

_____

_____

_____

Yr_____

_____

_____

_____

_____

_____

_____

_____

_____

16 MARCH

He who is destined for power does not have to fight for it. – African proverb

Yr_____

_____
_____
_____
_____
_____
_____
_____
_____

Yr_____

_____
_____
_____
_____
_____
_____
_____

Yr_____

_____
_____
_____
_____
_____
_____
_____

17 MARCH

Peace is costly but it is worth the expense. — African proverb

Yr_____

_____
_____
_____
_____
_____
_____
_____

Yr_____

_____
_____
_____
_____
_____
_____
_____

Yr_____

_____
_____
_____
_____
_____
_____
_____
_____

18 MARCH

A man who uses force is afraid of reasoning. — African proverb

Yr_____

_____
_____
_____
_____
_____
_____
_____

Yr_____

_____
_____
_____
_____
_____
_____
_____

Yr_____

_____
_____
_____
_____
_____
_____
_____
_____

19 MARCH

Wisdom is like fire. People take it from others. — African proverb

Yr_____

_____
_____
_____
_____
_____
_____
_____
_____

Yr_____

_____
_____
_____
_____
_____
_____
_____

Yr_____

_____
_____
_____
_____
_____
_____
_____
_____

20 MARCH

He that beats the drum for the mad man to dance is no better than the mad man himself. — African proverb

Yr_____

_____
_____
_____
_____
_____
_____
_____

Yr_____

_____
_____
_____
_____
_____
_____

Yr_____

_____
_____
_____
_____
_____
_____
_____

21 MARCH

Even the longest rope has an end. — African proverb

Yr_____

_____
_____
_____
_____
_____
_____
_____
_____

Yr_____

_____
_____
_____
_____
_____
_____
_____
_____

Yr_____

_____
_____
_____
_____
_____
_____
_____
_____

22 MARCH

If you find no fish, you have to eat bread – African proverb

Yr_____

_____

_____

_____

_____

_____

_____

_____

Yr_____

_____

_____

_____

_____

_____

_____

Yr_____

_____

_____

_____

_____

_____

_____

_____

23 MARCH

Where you will sit when you are old shows where you stood in your youth. – African proverb

Yr_____

_____
_____
_____
_____
_____
_____
_____

Yr_____

_____
_____
_____
_____
_____
_____
_____

Yr_____

_____
_____
_____
_____
_____
_____
_____
_____

24 MARCH

*If the rhythm of the drumbeats changes, the dance steps must adapt. –
African proverb*

Yr_____

_____
_____
_____
_____
_____
_____
_____

Yr_____

_____
_____
_____
_____
_____
_____

Yr_____

_____
_____
_____
_____
_____
_____
_____

25 MARCH

Even the lion, the king of the forest, protects himself against flies. –
African proverb

Yr_____

_____

_____

_____

_____

_____

_____

_____

Yr_____

_____

_____

_____

_____

_____

_____

_____

Yr_____

_____

_____

_____

_____

_____

_____

_____

26 MARCH

If you are filled with pride, then you will have no room for wisdom. –
African proverb

Yr_____

_____

_____

_____

_____

_____

_____

_____

Yr_____

_____

_____

_____

_____

_____

_____

_____

Yr_____

_____

_____

_____

_____

_____

_____

_____

27 MARCH

He who learns, teaches. — African proverb

Yr_____

_____

_____

_____

_____

_____

_____

_____

_____

Yr_____

_____

_____

_____

_____

_____

_____

_____

Yr_____

_____

_____

_____

_____

_____

_____

_____

_____

28 MARCH

Advice is a stranger; if he's welcome he stays for the night; if not, he leaves the same day. – African proverb

Yr_____

_____
_____
_____
_____
_____
_____
_____

Yr_____

_____
_____
_____
_____
_____
_____
_____

Yr_____

_____
_____
_____
_____
_____
_____
_____

29 MARCH

When a king has good counselors, his reign is peaceful. — African proverb

Yr_____

_____
_____
_____
_____
_____
_____
_____

Yr_____

_____
_____
_____
_____
_____
_____
_____

Yr_____

_____
_____
_____
_____
_____
_____
_____
_____

30 MARCH

If you can't resolve your problems in peace, you can't solve war. –
African proverb

Yr_____

_____
_____
_____
_____
_____
_____
_____

Yr_____

_____
_____
_____
_____
_____
_____
_____

Yr_____

_____
_____
_____
_____
_____
_____
_____
_____

31 MARCH

When two elephants fight, it is the grass that gets trampled. – African proverb

Yr_____

_____
_____
_____
_____
_____
_____
_____
_____

Yr_____

_____
_____
_____
_____
_____
_____
_____
_____

Yr_____

_____
_____
_____
_____
_____
_____
_____
_____
_____

1 APRIL

*A spider's cobweb isn't only its sleeping spring but also its food trap. —
African proverb*

Yr_____

_____

_____

_____

_____

_____

_____

_____

Yr_____

_____

_____

_____

_____

_____

_____

_____

Yr_____

_____

_____

_____

_____

_____

_____

_____

2 APRIL

If you pick up one end of the stick you also pick up the other. — African proverb

Yr_____

_____
_____
_____
_____
_____
_____
_____

Yr_____

_____
_____
_____
_____
_____
_____
_____

Yr_____

_____
_____
_____
_____
_____
_____
_____

3 APRIL

The young bird does not crow until it hears the old ones. - African proverb

Yr_____

_____
_____
_____
_____
_____
_____
_____

Yr_____

_____
_____
_____
_____
_____
_____

Yr_____

_____
_____
_____
_____
_____
_____
_____

4 APRIL

The night has ears. - African Proverb

Yr_____

_____

_____

_____

_____

_____

_____

_____

_____

Yr_____

_____

_____

_____

_____

_____

_____

_____

_____

Yr_____

_____

_____

_____

_____

_____

_____

_____

_____

5 APRIL

The worlds of the elders do not lock all the doors; they leave the right door open. – African Proverb

Yr_____

_____

_____

_____

_____

_____

_____

_____

Yr_____

_____

_____

_____

_____

_____

_____

_____

Yr_____

_____

_____

_____

_____

_____

_____

_____

6 APRIL

Birds sing not because they have answers but because they have songs.
— African proverb

Yr_____

_____
_____
_____
_____
_____
_____
_____

Yr_____

_____
_____
_____
_____
_____
_____
_____

Yr_____

_____
_____
_____
_____
_____
_____
_____

7 APRIL

One who bathes willingly with cold water doesn't feel the cold. —
African proverb

Yr_____

_____
_____
_____
_____
_____
_____
_____

Yr_____

_____
_____
_____
_____
_____
_____

Yr_____

_____
_____
_____
_____
_____
_____
_____

8 APRIL

When the roots of a tree begin to decay, it spreads death to the branches. – African proverb

Yr_____

_____
_____
_____
_____
_____
_____
_____
_____

Yr_____

_____
_____
_____
_____
_____
_____
_____

Yr_____

_____
_____
_____
_____
_____
_____
_____
_____

9 APRIL

An orphaned calf licks its own back. – African Proverb

Yr_____

_____

_____

_____

_____

_____

_____

Yr_____

_____

_____

_____

_____

_____

_____

Yr_____

_____

_____

_____

_____

_____

_____

_____

10 APRIL

Don't look where you fell, look where you slipped. — African proverb

Yr_____

_____

_____

_____

_____

_____

_____

_____

Yr_____

_____

_____

_____

_____

_____

_____

_____

Yr_____

_____

_____

_____

_____

_____

_____

_____

11 APRIL

A bird that flies off the earth and lands on an anthill is still on the ground. – African proverb

Yr_____

_____
_____
_____
_____
_____
_____
_____

Yr_____

_____
_____
_____
_____
_____
_____
_____

Yr_____

_____
_____
_____
_____
_____
_____
_____

12 APRIL

There is no beauty but the beauty of action. – African proverb

Yr_____

_____
_____
_____
_____
_____
_____
_____
_____

Yr_____

_____
_____
_____
_____
_____
_____
_____
_____

Yr_____

_____
_____
_____
_____
_____
_____
_____
_____
_____

13 APRIL

Wisdom is wealth. – African proverb

Yr_____

_____
_____
_____
_____
_____
_____
_____
_____

Yr_____

_____
_____
_____
_____
_____
_____
_____
_____

Yr_____

_____
_____
_____
_____
_____
_____
_____
_____

14 APRIL

If you close your eyes to facts, you will learn through accidents. –
African proverb

Yr_____

_____
_____
_____
_____
_____
_____
_____
_____

Yr_____

_____
_____
_____
_____
_____
_____
_____

Yr_____

_____
_____
_____
_____
_____
_____
_____
_____

15 APRIL

You cannot build a house for last year's summer. – African proverb

Yr_____

_____

_____

_____

_____

_____

_____

_____

Yr_____

_____

_____

_____

_____

_____

_____

Yr_____

_____

_____

_____

_____

_____

_____

_____

16 APRIL

However far a stream flows, it never forgets its origin. – African proverb

Yr_____

_____

_____

_____

_____

_____

_____

_____

_____

Yr_____

_____

_____

_____

_____

_____

_____

_____

Yr_____

_____

_____

_____

_____

_____

_____

_____

_____

17 APRIL

A wise person will always find a way. – African proverb

Yr_____

_____
_____
_____
_____
_____
_____
_____

Yr_____

_____
_____
_____
_____
_____
_____
_____

Yr_____

_____
_____
_____
_____
_____
_____
_____
_____

18 APRIL

By trying often, the monkey learns to jump from the tree. — African proverb

Yr_____

_____
_____
_____
_____
_____
_____
_____

Yr_____

_____
_____
_____
_____
_____
_____
_____

Yr_____

_____
_____
_____
_____
_____
_____
_____
_____

19 APRIL

What you help a child to love can be more important than what you help him to learn. – African proverb

Yr_____

_____
_____
_____
_____
_____
_____
_____

Yr_____

_____
_____
_____
_____
_____
_____

Yr_____

_____
_____
_____
_____
_____
_____
_____

20 APRIL

Where there are experts there will be no lack of learners. – African proverb

Yr_____

_____
_____
_____
_____
_____
_____
_____
_____

Yr_____

_____
_____
_____
_____
_____
_____
_____
_____

Yr_____

_____
_____
_____
_____
_____
_____
_____
_____

21 APRIL

Without a leader, black ants are confused. — African proverb

Yr_____

_____

_____

_____

_____

_____

_____

_____

Yr_____

_____

_____

_____

_____

_____

_____

_____

Yr_____

_____

_____

_____

_____

_____

_____

_____

22 APRIL

Cross the river in a crowd and the crocodile won't eat you. – African proverb

Yr_____

_____
_____
_____
_____
_____
_____
_____

Yr_____

_____
_____
_____
_____
_____
_____
_____

Yr_____

_____
_____
_____
_____
_____
_____
_____

23 APRIL

If you want to go quickly, go alone. If you want to go far, go together. –
African proverb

Yr_____

_____
_____
_____
_____
_____
_____
_____

Yr_____

_____
_____
_____
_____
_____
_____
_____

Yr_____

_____
_____
_____
_____
_____
_____
_____

24 APRIL

Home affairs are not talked about on the public square. — *African proverb*

Yr_____

_____

_____

_____

_____

_____

_____

_____

Yr_____

_____

_____

_____

_____

_____

_____

_____

Yr_____

_____

_____

_____

_____

_____

_____

_____

25 APRIL

Where a woman rules, streams run uphill. – African proverb

Yr_____

_____

_____

_____

_____

_____

_____

_____

Yr_____

_____

_____

_____

_____

_____

_____

_____

Yr_____

_____

_____

_____

_____

_____

_____

_____

_____

26 APRIL

Dine with a stranger but save your love for your family. — African proverb

Yr_____

_____
_____
_____
_____
_____
_____
_____
_____

Yr_____

_____
_____
_____
_____
_____
_____
_____
_____

Yr_____

_____
_____
_____
_____
_____
_____
_____
_____

27 APRIL

Hold a true friend with both hands. — African proverb

Yr_____

_____

_____

_____

_____

_____

_____

_____

Yr_____

_____

_____

_____

_____

_____

_____

_____

Yr_____

_____

_____

_____

_____

_____

_____

_____

_____

28 APRIL

He who loves money must labor. – African proverb

Yr_____

_____
_____
_____
_____
_____
_____
_____
_____
_____

Yr_____

_____
_____
_____
_____
_____
_____
_____
_____

Yr_____

_____
_____
_____
_____
_____
_____
_____
_____
_____

29 APRIL

Money is sharper than the sword. – African proverb

Yr_____

_____
_____
_____
_____
_____
_____
_____
_____

Yr_____

_____
_____
_____
_____
_____
_____
_____
_____

Yr_____

_____
_____
_____
_____
_____
_____
_____
_____

30 APRIL

Dogs do not actually prefer bones to meat; it is just that no one ever gives them meat. – African proverb

Yr_____

_____

_____

_____

_____

_____

_____

_____

Yr_____

_____

_____

_____

_____

_____

_____

_____

Yr_____

_____

_____

_____

_____

_____

_____

_____

1 MAY

A rolling stone gathers no moss. — African proverb

Yr_____

_____

_____

_____

_____

_____

_____

_____

_____

Yr_____

_____

_____

_____

_____

_____

_____

_____

_____

Yr_____

_____

_____

_____

_____

_____

_____

_____

_____

2 MAY

Knowledge without wisdom is like water in the sand. — African proverb

Yr_____

_____
_____
_____
_____
_____
_____
_____
_____

Yr_____

_____
_____
_____
_____
_____
_____
_____

Yr_____

_____
_____
_____
_____
_____
_____
_____
_____

3 MAY

Only witches get afraid when news spreads that the witch hunter is coming to town. - African proverb

Yr_____

_____

_____

_____

_____

_____

_____

_____

Yr_____

_____

_____

_____

_____

_____

_____

_____

Yr_____

_____

_____

_____

_____

_____

_____

_____

4 MAY

It is foolish to put your finger in someone's mouth and then hit them over the head. - African Proverb

Yr_____

_____

_____

_____

_____

_____

_____

_____

Yr_____

_____

_____

_____

_____

_____

_____

_____

Yr_____

_____

_____

_____

_____

_____

_____

_____

_____

5 MAY

What is for you will see your face. — African Proverb

Yr_____

_____
_____
_____
_____
_____
_____
_____
_____

Yr_____

_____
_____
_____
_____
_____
_____
_____
_____

Yr_____

_____
_____
_____
_____
_____
_____
_____
_____

6 MAY

When rain falls, it falls both on the master and the slave. — African proverb

Yr_____

_____

_____

_____

_____

_____

_____

_____

Yr_____

_____

_____

_____

_____

_____

_____

_____

Yr_____

_____

_____

_____

_____

_____

_____

_____

7 MAY

Between true friends even water drunk together is sweet enough. —
African proverb

Yr_____

_____
_____
_____
_____
_____
_____
_____
_____

Yr_____

_____
_____
_____
_____
_____
_____
_____
_____

Yr_____

_____
_____
_____
_____
_____
_____
_____
_____

8 MAY

Never argue with a fool, someone watching May not be able to tell the difference. – African proverb

Yr_____

_____
_____
_____
_____
_____
_____
_____

Yr_____

_____
_____
_____
_____
_____
_____
_____

Yr_____

_____
_____
_____
_____
_____
_____
_____
_____

9 MAY

When a man says yes, his chi (personal god) says yes also. – African Proverb

Yr_____

_____

_____

_____

_____

_____

_____

_____

Yr_____

_____

_____

_____

_____

_____

_____

_____

Yr_____

_____

_____

_____

_____

_____

_____

_____

10 MAY

No matter the economy of the jungle, lions will never eat grass. –
African proverb

Yr_____

_____
_____
_____
_____
_____
_____
_____
_____

Yr_____

_____
_____
_____
_____
_____
_____
_____

Yr_____

_____
_____
_____
_____
_____
_____
_____
_____

11 MAY

The load is lighter when two people carry it. – African proverb

Yr_____

_____

_____

_____

_____

_____

_____

_____

Yr_____

_____

_____

_____

_____

_____

_____

Yr_____

_____

_____

_____

_____

_____

_____

_____

_____

12 MAY

Those whose palm-kernels were cracked for them by a benevolent spirit should not forget to be humble. – African proverb

Yr_____

_____
_____
_____
_____
_____
_____
_____
_____

Yr_____

_____
_____
_____
_____
_____
_____
_____

Yr_____

_____
_____
_____
_____
_____
_____
_____
_____

13 MAY

The sun will shine on those who stand before it shines on those who kneel under them. – African proverb

Yr_____

_____

_____

_____

_____

_____

_____

Yr_____

_____

_____

_____

_____

_____

_____

Yr_____

_____

_____

_____

_____

_____

_____

14 MAY

People should not talk while they are eating or pepper May go down the wrong way. — African proverb

Yr_____

_____
_____
_____
_____
_____
_____
_____
_____

Yr_____

_____
_____
_____
_____
_____
_____
_____
_____

Yr_____

_____
_____
_____
_____
_____
_____
_____
_____
_____

15 MAY

A proud heart can survive a general failure because such a failure does not prick its pride. – African proverb

Yr_____

_____
_____
_____
_____
_____
_____
_____

Yr_____

_____
_____
_____
_____
_____
_____

Yr_____

_____
_____
_____
_____
_____
_____
_____

16 MAY

A man who pays respect to the great paves the way for his own greatness. – African proverb

Yr_____

_____
_____
_____
_____
_____
_____
_____

Yr_____

_____
_____
_____
_____
_____
_____
_____

Yr_____

_____
_____
_____
_____
_____
_____
_____
_____

17 MAY

One falsehood spoils a thousand truths. – African proverb

Yr_____

_____

_____

_____

_____

_____

_____

_____

Yr_____

_____

_____

_____

_____

_____

_____

_____

Yr_____

_____

_____

_____

_____

_____

_____

_____

18 MAY

A tree is straightened while it is still young. — African proverb

Yr_____

_____

_____

_____

_____

_____

_____

_____

Yr_____

_____

_____

_____

_____

_____

_____

Yr_____

_____

_____

_____

_____

_____

_____

_____

_____

19 MAY

Confiding a secret to an unworthy person is like carrying grain in a bag with a hole. – African proverb

Yr_____

_____

_____

_____

_____

_____

_____

_____

Yr_____

_____

_____

_____

_____

_____

_____

_____

Yr_____

_____

_____

_____

_____

_____

_____

_____

_____

20 MAY

He who does not know one thing knows another. – African proverb

Yr_____

_____

_____

_____

_____

_____

_____

_____

Yr_____

_____

_____

_____

_____

_____

_____

_____

Yr_____

_____

_____

_____

_____

_____

_____

_____

21 MAY

Rain does not fall on one roof alone. – African proverb

Yr_____

_____
_____
_____
_____
_____
_____
_____
_____

Yr_____

_____
_____
_____
_____
_____
_____
_____

Yr_____

_____
_____
_____
_____
_____
_____
_____
_____

22 MAY

However long the night May last, there will be a morning. — African proverb

Yr_____

_____
_____
_____
_____
_____
_____
_____

Yr_____

_____
_____
_____
_____
_____
_____

Yr_____

_____
_____
_____
_____
_____
_____
_____
_____

23 MAY

Smooth seas do not make skillful sailors. – African proverb

Yr_____

_____

_____

_____

_____

_____

_____

_____

Yr_____

_____

_____

_____

_____

_____

_____

_____

Yr_____

_____

_____

_____

_____

_____

_____

_____

_____

24 MAY

Lack of knowledge is darker than night. — African proverb

Yr_____

_____

Yr_____

_____

Yr_____

_____

25 MAY

If you are filled with pride, then you will have no room for wisdom. —
African proverb

Yr_____

_____

_____

_____

_____

_____

_____

_____

Yr_____

_____

_____

_____

_____

_____

_____

_____

Yr_____

_____

_____

_____

_____

_____

_____

_____

26 MAY

A single stick May smoke, but it will not burn. – African proverb

Yr_____

_____

_____

_____

_____

_____

_____

_____

_____

Yr_____

_____

_____

_____

_____

_____

_____

_____

Yr_____

_____

_____

_____

_____

_____

_____

_____

_____

27 MAY

If you offend, ask for a pardon; if offended forgive.   — African proverb

Yr_____

_____
_____
_____
_____
_____
_____
_____
_____

Yr_____

_____
_____
_____
_____
_____
_____
_____

Yr_____

_____
_____
_____
_____
_____
_____
_____
_____

28 MAY

Sticks in a bundle are unbreakable. – African proverb

Yr____

_____
_____
_____
_____
_____
_____
_____
_____

Yr____

_____
_____
_____
_____
_____
_____
_____

Yr____

_____
_____
_____
_____
_____
_____
_____
_____

29 MAY

He who thinks he is leading and has no one following him is only taking a walk. – African proverb

Yr_____

_____

_____

_____

_____

_____

_____

Yr_____

_____

_____

_____

_____

_____

_____

Yr_____

_____

_____

_____

_____

_____

_____

_____

30 MAY

If you climb up a tree, you must climb down the same tree. – African proverb

Yr_____

_____

_____

_____

_____

_____

_____

_____

Yr_____

_____

_____

_____

_____

_____

_____

_____

Yr_____

_____

_____

_____

_____

_____

_____

_____

31 MAY

An abundance of food at your neighbor's will not satisfy your hunger. –
African proverb

Yr_____

_____

_____

_____

_____

_____

_____

_____

Yr_____

_____

_____

_____

_____

_____

_____

_____

Yr_____

_____

_____

_____

_____

_____

_____

_____

1 JUNE

Lack of money is lack of friends; if you have money at your disposal, every dog and goat will claim to be related to you. — African proverb

Yr_____

_____
_____
_____
_____
_____
_____
_____

Yr_____

_____
_____
_____
_____
_____
_____
_____

Yr_____

_____
_____
_____
_____
_____
_____
_____

2 JUNE

A real family eats the same cornmeal.   — African proverb

Yr_____

_____

_____

_____

_____

_____

_____

_____

_____

Yr_____

_____

_____

_____

_____

_____

_____

_____

_____

Yr_____

_____

_____

_____

_____

_____

_____

_____

_____

_____

3 JUNE

He who receives a gift does not measure. - African proverb

Yr_____

Yr_____

Yr_____

4 JUNE

There is no one who became rich because he broke a holiday; no one became fat because he broke a fast. - African Proverb

Yr_____

_____
_____
_____
_____
_____
_____
_____

Yr_____

_____
_____
_____
_____
_____
_____

Yr_____

_____
_____
_____
_____
_____
_____
_____
_____

5 JUNE

Greed loses what it has gained. – African Proverb

Yr_____

_____
_____
_____
_____
_____
_____
_____
_____

Yr_____

_____
_____
_____
_____
_____
_____
_____
_____

Yr_____

_____
_____
_____
_____
_____
_____
_____
_____

6 JUNE

You must act as if it is impossible to fail. — African proverb

Yr_____

_____
_____
_____
_____
_____
_____
_____

Yr_____

_____
_____
_____
_____
_____
_____
_____

Yr_____

_____
_____
_____
_____
_____
_____
_____

7 JUNE

Ugliness with a good character is better than beauty. — African proverb

Yr_____

_____

_____

_____

_____

_____

_____

_____

Yr_____

_____

_____

_____

_____

_____

_____

Yr_____

_____

_____

_____

_____

_____

_____

_____

8 JUNE

You are beautiful because of your possessions. – African proverb

Yr_____

_____
_____
_____
_____
_____
_____
_____

Yr_____

_____
_____
_____
_____
_____
_____
_____

Yr_____

_____
_____
_____
_____
_____
_____
_____

9 JUNE

Three things cause sorrow to flee; water, green trees, and a beautiful face. – African Proverb

Yr_____

_____

_____

_____

_____

_____

_____

_____

Yr_____

_____

_____

_____

_____

_____

_____

_____

Yr_____

_____

_____

_____

_____

_____

_____

_____

_____

10 JUNE

It's those ugly caterpillars that turn into beautiful butterflies after seasons. – African proverb

Yr_____

_____

_____

_____

_____

_____

_____

_____

Yr_____

_____

_____

_____

_____

_____

_____

_____

Yr_____

_____

_____

_____

_____

_____

_____

_____

_____

11 JUNE

You are beautiful, but learn to work, for you cannot eat your beauty. —
African proverb

Yr_____

_____

_____

_____

_____

_____

_____

_____

Yr_____

_____

_____

_____

_____

_____

_____

_____

Yr_____

_____

_____

_____

_____

_____

_____

_____

12 JUNE

One thread for the needle, one love for the heart. – African proverb

Yr_____

_____
_____
_____
_____
_____
_____
_____
_____

Yr_____

_____
_____
_____
_____
_____
_____
_____

Yr_____

_____
_____
_____
_____
_____
_____
_____
_____

13 JUNE

Hurry, hurry has no blessings. — African proverb

Yr_____

_____

_____

_____

_____

_____

_____

_____

Yr_____

_____

_____

_____

_____

_____

_____

_____

Yr_____

_____

_____

_____

_____

_____

_____

_____

14 JUNE

To run is not necessarily to arrive. — African proverb

Yr_____

_____
_____
_____
_____
_____
_____
_____
_____

Yr_____

_____
_____
_____
_____
_____
_____
_____
_____

Yr_____

_____
_____
_____
_____
_____
_____
_____
_____

15 JUNE

The forest not only hides man's enemies but it's full of man's medicine, healing power and food. – African proverb

Yr_____

_____
_____
_____
_____
_____
_____
_____

Yr_____

_____
_____
_____
_____
_____
_____
_____

Yr_____

_____
_____
_____
_____
_____
_____
_____

16 JUNE

The chicken that digs for food will not sleep hungry. — African proverb

Yr_____

_____

_____

_____

_____

_____

_____

_____

Yr_____

_____

_____

_____

_____

_____

_____

Yr_____

_____

_____

_____

_____

_____

_____

_____

17 JUNE

You should know what's being cooked in the kitchen otherwise you might eat a forbidden food. – African proverb

Yr_____

_____

_____

_____

_____

_____

_____

_____

Yr_____

_____

_____

_____

_____

_____

_____

_____

Yr_____

_____

_____

_____

_____

_____

_____

_____

_____

18 JUNE

If you watch your pot, your food will not burn. — African proverb

Yr_____

_____
_____
_____
_____
_____
_____
_____

Yr_____

_____
_____
_____
_____
_____
_____

Yr_____

_____
_____
_____
_____
_____
_____
_____

19 JUNE

Even the best cooking pot will not produce food. – African proverb

Yr_____

_____
_____
_____
_____
_____
_____
_____
_____
_____

Yr_____

_____
_____
_____
_____
_____
_____
_____
_____

Yr_____

_____
_____
_____
_____
_____
_____
_____
_____

20 JUNE

You cannot tell a hungry child that you gave him food yesterday. –
African proverb

Yr_____

_____

_____

_____

_____

_____

_____

_____

Yr_____

_____

_____

_____

_____

_____

_____

_____

Yr_____

_____

_____

_____

_____

_____

_____

_____

21 JUNE

If you don't stand for something, you will fall for something. – African proverb

Yr_____

_____
_____
_____
_____
_____
_____
_____

Yr_____

_____
_____
_____
_____
_____
_____
_____

Yr_____

_____
_____
_____
_____
_____
_____
_____

22 JUNE

A chattering bird builds no nest. — African proverb

Yr_____

_____
_____
_____
_____
_____
_____
_____

Yr_____

_____
_____
_____
_____
_____
_____
_____

Yr_____

_____
_____
_____
_____
_____
_____
_____

23 JUNE

Repetition is the mother of knowledge. – African proverb

Yr____

_____
_____
_____
_____
_____
_____
_____
_____

Yr____

_____
_____
_____
_____
_____
_____
_____

Yr____

_____
_____
_____
_____
_____
_____
_____
_____

24 JUNE

Knowledge is like a garden: If it is not cultivated, it cannot be harvested. — African proverb

Yr_____

_____
_____
_____
_____
_____
_____
_____
_____

Yr_____

_____
_____
_____
_____
_____
_____
_____
_____

Yr_____

_____
_____
_____
_____
_____
_____
_____
_____

25 JUNE

He who digs a grave for another person, should be careful that he does not fall inside himself. — African proverb

Yr_____

_____
_____
_____
_____
_____
_____
_____

Yr_____

_____
_____
_____
_____
_____
_____
_____

Yr_____

_____
_____
_____
_____
_____
_____
_____

26 JUNE

What an old man sees sitting down, a young man cannot see even from the top of a tree. – African proverb

Yr_____

_____
_____
_____
_____
_____
_____
_____
_____

Yr_____

_____
_____
_____
_____
_____
_____
_____

Yr_____

_____
_____
_____
_____
_____
_____
_____
_____

27 JUNE

Wisdom is knowing what to do next; virtue is doing it. — African proverb

Yr_____

_____
_____
_____
_____
_____
_____
_____
_____

Yr_____

_____
_____
_____
_____
_____
_____
_____
_____

Yr_____

_____
_____
_____
_____
_____
_____
_____
_____
_____

28 JUNE

Looking at a king's mouth one would never think he sucked his mother's breast. – African proverb

Yr_____

_____

_____

_____

_____

_____

_____

_____

Yr_____

_____

_____

_____

_____

_____

_____

_____

Yr_____

_____

_____

_____

_____

_____

_____

_____

29 JUNE

If a child washes his hands he could eat with kings. — African proverb

Yr_____

_____
_____
_____
_____
_____
_____
_____
_____

Yr_____

_____
_____
_____
_____
_____
_____
_____

Yr_____

_____
_____
_____
_____
_____
_____
_____
_____

30 JUNE

You must attend to your business with the vendor in the market, and not to the noise of the market. – African proverb

Yr_____

_____

_____

_____

_____

_____

_____

_____

Yr_____

_____

_____

_____

_____

_____

_____

_____

Yr_____

_____

_____

_____

_____

_____

_____

_____

1 JULY

He who doesn't clean his mouth before breakfast always complains that the food is sour. — African proverb

Yr_____

_____
_____
_____
_____
_____
_____
_____

Yr_____

_____
_____
_____
_____
_____
_____

Yr_____

_____
_____
_____
_____
_____
_____
_____

2 JULY

It's much easier to fall in love than to stay in love. — African proverb

Yr_____

_____

_____

_____

_____

_____

_____

_____

Yr_____

_____

_____

_____

_____

_____

_____

_____

Yr_____

_____

_____

_____

_____

_____

_____

_____

3 JULY

When the shepherd comes home in peace, the milk is sweet. - African proverb

Yr_____

_____

_____

_____

_____

_____

_____

Yr_____

_____

_____

_____

_____

_____

_____

Yr_____

_____

_____

_____

_____

_____

_____

_____

4 JULY

If you do not have patience you cannot make beer. - African Proverb

Yr_____

_____
_____
_____
_____
_____
_____
_____

Yr_____

_____
_____
_____
_____
_____
_____
_____

Yr_____

_____
_____
_____
_____
_____
_____
_____
_____

5 JULY

He who runs after good fortune runs away from peace. — African Proverb

Yr_____

_____
_____
_____
_____
_____
_____
_____
_____

Yr_____

_____
_____
_____
_____
_____
_____
_____

Yr_____

_____
_____
_____
_____
_____
_____
_____
_____

6 JULY

Teeth do not see poverty .— African proverb

Yr_____

_____

_____

_____

_____

_____

_____

_____

Yr_____

_____

_____

_____

_____

_____

_____

_____

Yr_____

_____

_____

_____

_____

_____

_____

_____

_____

7 JULY

You have little power over what's not yours. — African proverb

Yr_____

_____

_____

_____

_____

_____

_____

_____

Yr_____

_____

_____

_____

_____

_____

_____

_____

Yr_____

_____

_____

_____

_____

_____

_____

_____

_____

8 JULY

Better little than too little. – African proverb

Yr_____

_____
_____
_____
_____
_____
_____
_____

Yr_____

_____
_____
_____
_____
_____
_____
_____

Yr_____

_____
_____
_____
_____
_____
_____
_____
_____

9 JULY

When you befriend a chief remember that he sits on a rope. — African Proverb

Yr_____

_____

_____

_____

_____

_____

_____

_____

Yr_____

_____

_____

_____

_____

_____

_____

_____

Yr_____

_____

_____

_____

_____

_____

_____

_____

10 JULY

The child you sired hasn't sired you. — African proverb

Yr_____

_____

_____

_____

_____

_____

_____

_____

Yr_____

_____

_____

_____

_____

_____

_____

_____

Yr_____

_____

_____

_____

_____

_____

_____

_____

_____

11 JULY

A doctor who invoked a storm on his people cannot prevent his house from destruction. – African proverb

Yr____

_____
_____
_____
_____
_____
_____
_____

Yr____

_____
_____
_____
_____
_____
_____
_____

Yr____

_____
_____
_____
_____
_____
_____
_____
_____

12 JULY

An intelligent enemy is better than a stupid friend. – African proverb

Yr_____

_____
_____
_____
_____
_____
_____
_____
_____

Yr_____

_____
_____
_____
_____
_____
_____
_____
_____

Yr_____

_____
_____
_____
_____
_____
_____
_____
_____

13 JULY

If you carry the egg basket do not dance. – African proverb

Yr_____

_____

_____

_____

_____

_____

_____

_____

_____

Yr_____

_____

_____

_____

_____

_____

_____

_____

_____

Yr_____

_____

_____

_____

_____

_____

_____

_____

_____

14 JULY

The food which is prepared has no master. – African proverb

Yr_____

_____

_____

_____

_____

_____

_____

_____

Yr_____

_____

_____

_____

_____

_____

_____

_____

Yr_____

_____

_____

_____

_____

_____

_____

_____

15 JULY

Do a good deed and throw it into the sea. — African proverb

Yr_____

_____
_____
_____
_____
_____
_____
_____

Yr_____

_____
_____
_____
_____
_____
_____
_____

Yr_____

_____
_____
_____
_____
_____
_____
_____

16 JULY

Slander by the stream will be heard by the frogs. — African proverb

Yr_____

_____
_____
_____
_____
_____
_____
_____
_____

Yr_____

_____
_____
_____
_____
_____
_____
_____
_____

Yr_____

_____
_____
_____
_____
_____
_____
_____
_____

17 JULY

A child is a child of everyone. – African proverb

Yr_____

_____

_____

_____

_____

_____

_____

_____

_____

Yr_____

_____

_____

_____

_____

_____

_____

_____

_____

Yr_____

_____

_____

_____

_____

_____

_____

_____

_____

_____

18 JULY

Even the best cooking pot will not produce food. — *African proverb*

Yr_____

_____
_____
_____
_____
_____
_____
_____

Yr_____

_____
_____
_____
_____
_____
_____
_____

Yr_____

_____
_____
_____
_____
_____
_____
_____

19 JULY

The child of a rat is a rat. – African proverb

Yr_____

_____
_____
_____
_____
_____
_____
_____
_____

Yr_____

_____
_____
_____
_____
_____
_____
_____
_____

Yr_____

_____
_____
_____
_____
_____
_____
_____
_____

20 JULY

If your only tool is a hammer, you will see every problem as a nail. –
African proverb

Yr_____

_____

_____

_____

_____

_____

_____

_____

Yr_____

_____

_____

_____

_____

_____

_____

_____

Yr_____

_____

_____

_____

_____

_____

_____

_____

_____

21 JULY

It is crooked wood that shows the best sculptor. – African proverb

Yr____

_____

_____

_____

_____

_____

_____

_____

Yr____

_____

_____

_____

_____

_____

_____

_____

Yr____

_____

_____

_____

_____

_____

_____

_____

22 JULY

Be a mountain or lean on one. — African proverb

Yr_____

_____

_____

_____

_____

_____

_____

_____

Yr_____

_____

_____

_____

_____

_____

_____

Yr_____

_____

_____

_____

_____

_____

_____

_____

23 JULY

Do not follow a person who is running away. – African proverb

Yr_____

_____
_____
_____
_____
_____
_____
_____
_____

Yr_____

_____
_____
_____
_____
_____
_____
_____
_____

Yr_____

_____
_____
_____
_____
_____
_____
_____
_____

24 JULY

He who burns down his house knows why ashes cost a fortune. — African proverb

Yr_____

_____
_____
_____
_____
_____
_____
_____

Yr_____

_____
_____
_____
_____
_____
_____
_____

Yr_____

_____
_____
_____
_____
_____
_____
_____
_____

25 JULY

*We desire to bequeath two things to our children; the first one is roots,
the other one is wings. – African proverb*

Yr_____

_____
_____
_____
_____
_____
_____
_____
_____

Yr_____

_____
_____
_____
_____
_____
_____
_____
_____

Yr_____

_____
_____
_____
_____
_____
_____
_____
_____

26 JULY

A lie has many variations, the truth none. – African proverb

Yr_____

Yr_____

Yr_____

27 JULY

The axe forgets but the tree remembers. – African proverb

Yr___

_____

_____

_____

_____

_____

_____

_____

Yr___

_____

_____

_____

_____

_____

_____

Yr___

_____

_____

_____

_____

_____

_____

_____

28 JULY

The death of an elderly man is like a burning library. – African proverb

Yr_____

_____

_____

_____

_____

_____

_____

_____

Yr_____

_____

_____

_____

_____

_____

_____

_____

Yr_____

_____

_____

_____

_____

_____

_____

_____

_____

29 JULY

Earth is the queen of beds. – African proverb

Yr_____

_____
_____
_____
_____
_____
_____
_____

Yr_____

_____
_____
_____
_____
_____
_____
_____

Yr_____

_____
_____
_____
_____
_____
_____
_____
_____

30 JULY

Don't set sail on someone else's star. – African proverb

Yr_____

_____

_____

_____

_____

_____

_____

_____

Yr_____

_____

_____

_____

_____

_____

_____

_____

Yr_____

_____

_____

_____

_____

_____

_____

_____

31 JULY

No person is born great. Great people become great when others are sleeping. — African proverb

Yr_____

_____

_____

_____

_____

_____

_____

_____

Yr_____

_____

_____

_____

_____

_____

_____

_____

Yr_____

_____

_____

_____

_____

_____

_____

_____

_____

1 AUGUST

The rooster belongs to one household, but when it crows it is heard by the entire village. — African proverb

Yr_____

_____
_____
_____
_____
_____
_____
_____
_____

Yr_____

_____
_____
_____
_____
_____
_____
_____
_____

Yr_____

_____
_____
_____
_____
_____
_____
_____
_____

2 AUGUST

If you give bad food to your stomach, it will drum for you to dance. —
African proverb

Yr_____

_____
_____
_____
_____
_____
_____
_____

Yr_____

_____
_____
_____
_____
_____
_____
_____

Yr_____

_____
_____
_____
_____
_____
_____
_____
_____

3 AUGUST

Silence is also a form of speech. - African proverb

Yr_____

_____

_____

_____

_____

_____

_____

_____

Yr_____

_____

_____

_____

_____

_____

_____

_____

Yr_____

_____

_____

_____

_____

_____

_____

_____

_____

4 AUGUST

A doctor who invoked a storm on his people cannot prevent his house from destruction. - African Proverb

Yr_____

_____
_____
_____
_____
_____
_____
_____
_____

Yr_____

_____
_____
_____
_____
_____
_____
_____

Yr_____

_____
_____
_____
_____
_____
_____
_____
_____

5 AUGUST

You must attend to your business with the vendor in the market, and not to the noise of the market. – African Proverb

Yr_____

_____
_____
_____
_____
_____
_____
_____

Yr_____

_____
_____
_____
_____
_____
_____

Yr_____

_____
_____
_____
_____
_____
_____
_____
_____

6 AUGUST

You can tell a ripe corn by its look. — African proverb

Yr_____

_____

_____

_____

_____

_____

_____

_____

_____

Yr_____

_____

_____

_____

_____

_____

_____

_____

_____

Yr_____

_____

_____

_____

_____

_____

_____

_____

_____

7 AUGUST

The lizard that jumped from the high iroko tree to the ground said he would praise himself if no one else did. — African proverb

Yr_____

_____
_____
_____
_____
_____
_____
_____
_____

Yr_____

_____
_____
_____
_____
_____
_____
_____

Yr_____

_____
_____
_____
_____
_____
_____
_____
_____

8 AUGUST

If you don't stand for something, you will fall for something. – African proverb

Yr_____

_____
_____
_____
_____
_____
_____
_____

Yr_____

_____
_____
_____
_____
_____
_____
_____

Yr_____

_____
_____
_____
_____
_____
_____
_____
_____

9 AUGUST

A wise man who knows proverbs, reconciles difficulties. – African Proverb

Yr_____

_____

_____

_____

_____

_____

_____

_____

Yr_____

_____

_____

_____

_____

_____

_____

_____

Yr_____

_____

_____

_____

_____

_____

_____

_____

_____

10 AUGUST

As the dog said, 'If I fall down for you and you fall down for me, it is playing.' — African proverb

Yr_____

_____
_____
_____
_____
_____
_____
_____

Yr_____

_____
_____
_____
_____
_____
_____
_____

Yr_____

_____
_____
_____
_____
_____
_____
_____
_____

11 AUGUST

A child's fingers are not scalded by a piece of hot yam which his mother puts into his palm. – African proverb

Yr_____

_____
_____
_____
_____
_____
_____
_____
_____

Yr_____

_____
_____
_____
_____
_____
_____
_____

Yr_____

_____
_____
_____
_____
_____
_____
_____
_____

12 AUGUST

A chick that will grow into a cock can be spotted the very day it hatches.
– African proverb

Yr_____

_____
_____
_____
_____
_____
_____
_____

Yr_____

_____
_____
_____
_____
_____
_____
_____

Yr_____

_____
_____
_____
_____
_____
_____
_____
_____
_____

13 AUGUST

A feeble effort will not fulfill the self. – African proverb

Yr_____

_____
_____
_____
_____
_____
_____
_____
_____

Yr_____

_____
_____
_____
_____
_____
_____
_____

Yr_____

_____
_____
_____
_____
_____
_____
_____
_____

14 AUGUST

When God cooks, you don't see smoke. — African proverb

Yr_____

_____
_____
_____
_____
_____
_____
_____

Yr_____

_____
_____
_____
_____
_____
_____
_____

Yr_____

_____
_____
_____
_____
_____
_____
_____
_____
_____

15 AUGUST

The earth is a beehive, we all enter by the same door. – African proverb

Yr_____

_____

_____

_____

_____

_____

_____

Yr_____

_____

_____

_____

_____

_____

_____

Yr_____

_____

_____

_____

_____

_____

_____

_____

16 AUGUST

A friend is someone you share the path with. – African proverb

Yr_____

_____

_____

_____

_____

_____

_____

_____

Yr_____

_____

_____

_____

_____

_____

_____

_____

Yr_____

_____

_____

_____

_____

_____

_____

_____

17 AUGUST

When there is no enemy within, the enemies outside cannot hurt you. –
African proverb

Yr_____

_____

_____

_____

_____

_____

_____

_____

Yr_____

_____

_____

_____

_____

_____

_____

_____

Yr_____

_____

_____

_____

_____

_____

_____

_____

18 AUGUST

Having a good discussion is like having riches. — African proverb

Yr_____

_____
_____
_____
_____
_____
_____
_____
_____

Yr_____

_____
_____
_____
_____
_____
_____
_____
_____

Yr_____

_____
_____
_____
_____
_____
_____
_____
_____

19 AUGUST

By labor comes wealth. — African proverb

Yr_____

_____
_____
_____
_____
_____
_____
_____
_____

Yr_____

_____
_____
_____
_____
_____
_____
_____
_____

Yr_____

_____
_____
_____
_____
_____
_____
_____
_____
_____

20 AUGUST

He who is being carried does not realize how far the town is. – African proverb

Yr_____

_____
_____
_____
_____
_____
_____
_____

Yr_____

_____
_____
_____
_____
_____
_____
_____

Yr_____

_____
_____
_____
_____
_____
_____
_____
_____

21 AUGUST

One must talk little and listen much. – African proverb

Yr_____

_____

_____

_____

_____

_____

_____

Yr_____

_____

_____

_____

_____

_____

_____

Yr_____

_____

_____

_____

_____

_____

_____

_____

22 AUGUST

Wood already touched by fire is not hard to set alight. — African proverb

Yr_____

_____

_____

_____

_____

_____

_____

_____

Yr_____

_____

_____

_____

_____

_____

_____

_____

Yr_____

_____

_____

_____

_____

_____

_____

_____

_____

23 AUGUST

Do not call to a dog with a whip in your hand. — African proverb

Yr_____

_____

_____

_____

_____

_____

_____

_____

Yr_____

_____

_____

_____

_____

_____

_____

_____

Yr_____

_____

_____

_____

_____

_____

_____

_____

_____

24 AUGUST

A man who pays respect to the great paves his own way for greatness. –
African proverb

Yr_____

_____
_____
_____
_____
_____
_____
_____

Yr_____

_____
_____
_____
_____
_____
_____
_____

Yr_____

_____
_____
_____
_____
_____
_____
_____

25 AUGUST

A ripe melon falls by itself. – African proverb

Yr_____

_____

_____

_____

_____

_____

_____

_____

Yr_____

_____

_____

_____

_____

_____

_____

_____

Yr_____

_____

_____

_____

_____

_____

_____

_____

_____

26 AUGUST

Every misfortune is a blessing. – African proverb

Yr_____

_____

_____

_____

_____

_____

_____

_____

_____

Yr_____

_____

_____

_____

_____

_____

_____

_____

Yr_____

_____

_____

_____

_____

_____

_____

_____

_____

27 AUGUST

Even the mightiest eagle comes down to the tree tops to rest. – African proverb

Yr_____

_____

_____

_____

_____

_____

_____

_____

Yr_____

_____

_____

_____

_____

_____

_____

_____

Yr_____

_____

_____

_____

_____

_____

_____

_____

_____

28 AUGUST

There is no medicine to cure hatred. – African proverb

Yr_____

_____
_____
_____
_____
_____
_____
_____

Yr_____

_____
_____
_____
_____
_____
_____

Yr_____

_____
_____
_____
_____
_____
_____
_____
_____

29 AUGUST

If you want to go quickly, go alone. If you want to go far, go together. –
African proverb

Yr____

_____
_____
_____
_____
_____
_____
_____

Yr____

_____
_____
_____
_____
_____
_____

Yr____

_____
_____
_____
_____
_____
_____
_____

30 AUGUST

It is not work that kills, but worry. – African proverb

Yr_____

_____

_____

_____

_____

_____

_____

_____

_____

Yr_____

_____

_____

_____

_____

_____

_____

_____

_____

Yr_____

_____

_____

_____

_____

_____

_____

_____

_____

31 JULY

It is not what you are called, but what you answer to. – African proverb

Yr_____

_____

_____

_____

_____

_____

_____

_____

_____

Yr_____

_____

_____

_____

_____

_____

_____

_____

_____

Yr_____

_____

_____

_____

_____

_____

_____

_____

_____

1 SEPTEMBER

Merely wishing to fly will not enable one to fly. Doing what one really can do is much more fruitful than wishful thinking. — African proverb

Yr_____

_____

_____

_____

_____

_____

_____

_____

Yr_____

_____

_____

_____

_____

_____

_____

_____

Yr_____

_____

_____

_____

_____

_____

_____

_____

2 SEPTEMBER

One who bears a male child bears on person—perhaps a great warrior, or a prince, a griot. But one who bears a female child bears a who village—a nation, a kingdom, the world. — African proverb

Yr_____

_____
_____
_____
_____
_____
_____
_____

Yr_____

_____
_____
_____
_____
_____
_____
_____

Yr_____

_____
_____
_____
_____
_____
_____
_____
_____

3 SEPTEMBER

An honest man is he who not just talks honesty but lives honesty. -
African proverb

Yr_____

_____
_____
_____
_____
_____
_____
_____

Yr_____

_____
_____
_____
_____
_____
_____
_____

Yr_____

_____
_____
_____
_____
_____
_____
_____

4 SEPTEMBER

Even the lion, the king of the forest, protects himself against flies. -
African Proverb

Yr_____

_____
_____
_____
_____
_____
_____
_____

Yr_____

_____
_____
_____
_____
_____
_____
_____

Yr_____

_____
_____
_____
_____
_____
_____
_____
_____

5 SEPTEMBER

Wisdom is like a baobab tree; no one individual can embrace it. — African Proverb

Yr_____

_____
_____
_____
_____
_____
_____
_____

Yr_____

_____
_____
_____
_____
_____
_____
_____

Yr_____

_____
_____
_____
_____
_____
_____
_____
_____

6 SEPTEMBER

If you think you're too small to make a difference, spend a night with a mosquito. — African proverb

Yr_____

_____
_____
_____
_____
_____
_____
_____

Yr_____

_____
_____
_____
_____
_____
_____
_____

Yr_____

_____
_____
_____
_____
_____
_____
_____

7 SEPTEMBER

If there is no enemy within, the enemy outside can do no harm. —
African proverb

Yr_____

_____
_____
_____
_____
_____
_____
_____
_____

Yr_____

_____
_____
_____
_____
_____
_____
_____
_____

Yr_____

_____
_____
_____
_____
_____
_____
_____
_____

8 SEPTEMBER

When elephants fight, it's the grass that suffers. — African proverb

Yr_____

_____
_____
_____
_____
_____
_____
_____

Yr_____

_____
_____
_____
_____
_____
_____

Yr_____

_____
_____
_____
_____
_____
_____
_____
_____

9 SEPTEMBER

Even the longest rope has an end. – African Proverb

Yr_____

_____
_____
_____
_____
_____
_____
_____
_____

Yr_____

_____
_____
_____
_____
_____
_____
_____

Yr_____

_____
_____
_____
_____
_____
_____
_____
_____

10 SEPTEMBER

If you marry a monkey for his wealth, the money goes and the monkey remains as is. — African proverb

Yr_____

_____
_____
_____
_____
_____
_____
_____

Yr_____

_____
_____
_____
_____
_____
_____
_____

Yr_____

_____
_____
_____
_____
_____
_____
_____

11 SEPTEMBER

Wisdom is like a baobab tree, no one individual can embrace it. —
African proverb

Yr_____

_____
_____
_____
_____
_____
_____
_____
_____

Yr_____

_____
_____
_____
_____
_____
_____
_____
_____

Yr_____

_____
_____
_____
_____
_____
_____
_____
_____

12 SEPTEMBER

Where water is the boss, there the land must obey. – African proverb

Yr_____

_____
_____
_____
_____
_____
_____
_____
_____

Yr_____

_____
_____
_____
_____
_____
_____
_____

Yr_____

_____
_____
_____
_____
_____
_____
_____
_____

13 SEPTEMBER

An intelligent enemy is better than a stupid friend. – African proverb

Yr_____

_____
_____
_____
_____
_____
_____
_____

Yr_____

_____
_____
_____
_____
_____
_____
_____

Yr_____

_____
_____
_____
_____
_____
_____
_____
_____

14 SEPTEMBER

When you show the moon to a child, it sees only your finger. — African proverb

Yr_____

_____
_____
_____
_____
_____
_____
_____
_____

Yr_____

_____
_____
_____
_____
_____
_____
_____

Yr_____

_____
_____
_____
_____
_____
_____
_____
_____

15 SEPTEMBER

We desire to bequeath two things to our children: the first one is roots, the other one is wings. – African proverb

Yr_____

_____
_____
_____
_____
_____
_____
_____
_____

Yr_____

_____
_____
_____
_____
_____
_____
_____
_____

Yr_____

_____
_____
_____
_____
_____
_____
_____
_____
_____

16 SEPTEMBER

There can be no peace without understanding. – African proverb

Yr_____

_____
_____
_____
_____
_____
_____
_____
_____

Yr_____

_____
_____
_____
_____
_____
_____
_____
_____

Yr_____

_____
_____
_____
_____
_____
_____
_____
_____

17 SEPTEMBER

You learn how to cut down trees by cutting them down. – African proverb

Yr_____

_____
_____
_____
_____
_____
_____
_____

Yr_____

_____
_____
_____
_____
_____
_____
_____

Yr_____

_____
_____
_____
_____
_____
_____
_____

18 SEPTEMBER

Love is a despot who spares no one. — African proverb

Yr_____

_____
_____
_____
_____
_____
_____
_____
_____

Yr_____

_____
_____
_____
_____
_____
_____
_____

Yr_____

_____
_____
_____
_____
_____
_____
_____
_____

19 SEPTEMBER

Money is not the medicine against death. – African proverb

Yr_____

_____
_____
_____
_____
_____
_____
_____

Yr_____

_____
_____
_____
_____
_____
_____
_____

Yr_____

_____
_____
_____
_____
_____
_____
_____
_____

20 SEPTEMBER

The friends of our friends are our friends. — African proverb

Yr_____

_____

_____

_____

_____

_____

_____

_____

Yr_____

_____

_____

_____

_____

_____

_____

_____

Yr_____

_____

_____

_____

_____

_____

_____

_____

_____

21 SEPTEMBER

Two ants do not fail to pull one grasshopper. — African proverb

Yr_____

Yr_____

Yr_____

22 SEPTEMBER

The wealth which enslaves the owner isn't wealth. — African proverb

Yr_____

_____
_____
_____
_____
_____
_____
_____
_____

Yr_____

_____
_____
_____
_____
_____
_____
_____
_____

Yr_____

_____
_____
_____
_____
_____
_____
_____
_____

23 SEPTEMBER

The fool speaks, the wise man listens. — African proverb

Yr_____

_____
_____
_____
_____
_____
_____
_____
_____

Yr_____

_____
_____
_____
_____
_____
_____
_____

Yr_____

_____
_____
_____
_____
_____
_____
_____
_____

24 SEPTEMBER

Wisdom does not come overnight. — African proverb

Yr_____

_____
_____
_____
_____
_____
_____
_____

Yr_____

_____
_____
_____
_____
_____
_____
_____

Yr_____

_____
_____
_____
_____
_____
_____
_____

25 SEPTEMBER

The heart of the wise man lies quiet like limpid water. – African proverb

Yr_____

_____
_____
_____
_____
_____
_____
_____
_____

Yr_____

_____
_____
_____
_____
_____
_____
_____

Yr_____

_____
_____
_____
_____
_____
_____
_____
_____

26 SEPTEMBER

Only a wise person can solve a difficult problem. – African proverb

Yr_____

_____
_____
_____
_____
_____
_____
_____
_____

Yr_____

_____
_____
_____
_____
_____
_____
_____

Yr_____

_____
_____
_____
_____
_____
_____
_____
_____

27 SEPTEMBER

In the moment of crisis, the wise build bridges and the foolish build dams. — African proverb

Yr_____

_____
_____
_____
_____
_____
_____
_____

Yr_____

_____
_____
_____
_____
_____
_____
_____

Yr_____

_____
_____
_____
_____
_____
_____
_____

28 SEPTEMBER

Nobody is born wise. – African proverb

Yr_____

_____
_____
_____
_____
_____
_____
_____
_____

Yr_____

_____
_____
_____
_____
_____
_____
_____

Yr_____

_____
_____
_____
_____
_____
_____
_____
_____

29 SEPTEMBER

Learning expands great souls. — African proverb

Yr_____

_____
_____
_____
_____
_____
_____
_____
_____

Yr_____

_____
_____
_____
_____
_____
_____
_____
_____

Yr_____

_____
_____
_____
_____
_____
_____
_____
_____
_____

30 SEPTEMBER

By crawling a child learns to stand. – African proverb

Yr_____

_____
_____
_____
_____
_____
_____
_____

Yr_____

_____
_____
_____
_____
_____
_____

Yr_____

_____
_____
_____
_____
_____
_____
_____

1 OCTOBER

Seeing is different than being told. — African proverb

Yr_____

_____

_____

_____

_____

_____

_____

_____

Yr_____

_____

_____

_____

_____

_____

_____

_____

Yr_____

_____

_____

_____

_____

_____

_____

_____

2 OCTOBER

He who learns, teaches. — African proverb

Yr_____

_____

_____

_____

_____

_____

_____

_____

Yr_____

_____

_____

_____

_____

_____

_____

Yr_____

_____

_____

_____

_____

_____

_____

_____

3 OCTOBER

Ugliness with a good character is better than beauty. - African proverb

Yr_____

_____
_____
_____
_____
_____
_____
_____

Yr_____

_____
_____
_____
_____
_____
_____
_____

Yr_____

_____
_____
_____
_____
_____
_____
_____

4 OCTOBER

A good deed is something one returns. - African Proverb

Yr_____

_____

_____

_____

_____

_____

_____

_____

Yr_____

_____

_____

_____

_____

_____

_____

_____

Yr_____

_____

_____

_____

_____

_____

_____

_____

_____

5 OCTOBER

To try and to fail is not laziness. – African Proverb

Yr_____

_____
_____
_____
_____
_____
_____
_____
_____

Yr_____

_____
_____
_____
_____
_____
_____
_____

Yr_____

_____
_____
_____
_____
_____
_____
_____
_____

6 OCTOBER

Tomorrow belongs to the people who prepare for it today. — African proverb

Yr_____

_____
_____
_____
_____
_____
_____
_____

Yr_____

_____
_____
_____
_____
_____
_____
_____

Yr_____

_____
_____
_____
_____
_____
_____
_____

7 OCTOBER

You have little power over what's not yours. — African proverb

Yr_____

_____
_____
_____
_____
_____
_____
_____

Yr_____

_____
_____
_____
_____
_____
_____
_____

Yr_____

_____
_____
_____
_____
_____
_____
_____
_____

8 OCTOBER

Do not follow a person who is running away. – African proverb

Yr_____

_____

_____

_____

_____

_____

_____

_____

Yr_____

_____

_____

_____

_____

_____

_____

_____

Yr_____

_____

_____

_____

_____

_____

_____

_____

_____

9 OCTOBER

Even the best cooking pot will not produce food. – African Proverb

Yr_____

_____
_____
_____
_____
_____
_____
_____
_____

Yr_____

_____
_____
_____
_____
_____
_____
_____

Yr_____

_____
_____
_____
_____
_____
_____
_____
_____

10 OCTOBER

If you run after two hares you will catch neither. — African proverb

Yr_____

_____
_____
_____
_____
_____
_____
_____
_____

Yr_____

_____
_____
_____
_____
_____
_____
_____
_____

Yr_____

_____
_____
_____
_____
_____
_____
_____
_____

11 OCTOBER

If you see a man in a gown eating with a man in rags, the food belongs to the latter. – African proverb

Yr____

_____

_____

_____

_____

_____

_____

_____

Yr____

_____

_____

_____

_____

_____

_____

_____

Yr____

_____

_____

_____

_____

_____

_____

_____

12 OCTOBER

When your luck deserts you, even cold food burns. – African proverb

Yr_____

_____
_____
_____
_____
_____
_____
_____

Yr_____

_____
_____
_____
_____
_____
_____
_____

Yr_____

_____
_____
_____
_____
_____
_____
_____
_____

13 OCTOBER

He who fears the sun will not become chief. – African proverb

Yr_____

_____

_____

_____

_____

_____

_____

_____

Yr_____

_____

_____

_____

_____

_____

_____

_____

Yr_____

_____

_____

_____

_____

_____

_____

_____

_____

14 OCTOBER

An army of sheep led by a lion can defeat an army of lions led by a sheep. — African proverb

Yr_____

_____
_____
_____
_____
_____
_____
_____

Yr_____

_____
_____
_____
_____
_____
_____
_____

Yr_____

_____
_____
_____
_____
_____
_____
_____

15 OCTOBER

When there is peace in the country, the chief does not carry a shield. –
African proverb

Yr_____

_____
_____
_____
_____
_____
_____
_____
_____

Yr_____

_____
_____
_____
_____
_____
_____
_____
_____

Yr_____

_____
_____
_____
_____
_____
_____
_____
_____

16 OCTOBER

Milk and honey have different colors, but they share the same house peacefully. – African proverb

Yr_____

_____

_____

_____

_____

_____

_____

_____

Yr_____

_____

_____

_____

_____

_____

_____

Yr_____

_____

_____

_____

_____

_____

_____

_____

17 OCTOBER

There can be no peace without understanding. — African proverb

Yr_____

_____
_____
_____
_____
_____
_____
_____
_____

Yr_____

_____
_____
_____
_____
_____
_____
_____
_____

Yr_____

_____
_____
_____
_____
_____
_____
_____
_____

18 OCTOBER

Peace does not make a good ruler. — African proverb

Yr_____

_____
_____
_____
_____
_____
_____
_____

Yr_____

_____
_____
_____
_____
_____
_____

Yr_____

_____
_____
_____
_____
_____
_____
_____
_____

19 OCTOBER

War has no eyes. – African proverb

Yr_____

_____
_____
_____
_____
_____
_____
_____

Yr_____

_____
_____
_____
_____
_____
_____
_____

Yr_____

_____
_____
_____
_____
_____
_____
_____
_____

20 OCTOBER

Ears that do not listen to advice, accompany the head when it is chopped off. – African proverb

Yr_____

_____
_____
_____
_____
_____
_____
_____
_____

Yr_____

_____
_____
_____
_____
_____
_____

Yr_____

_____
_____
_____
_____
_____
_____
_____

21 OCTOBER

You do not teach the paths of the forest to an old gorilla. — African proverb

Yr_____

_____
_____
_____
_____
_____
_____
_____

Yr_____

_____
_____
_____
_____
_____
_____
_____

Yr_____

_____
_____
_____
_____
_____
_____
_____

22 OCTOBER

The wise create proverbs for fools to learn, not to repeat. — African proverb

Yr_____

_____
_____
_____
_____
_____
_____
_____

Yr_____

_____
_____
_____
_____
_____
_____

Yr_____

_____
_____
_____
_____
_____
_____
_____

23 OCTOBER

You always learn a lot more when you lose than when you win. – African proverb

Yr_____

_____
_____
_____
_____
_____
_____
_____
_____

Yr_____

_____
_____
_____
_____
_____
_____
_____
_____

Yr_____

_____
_____
_____
_____
_____
_____
_____
_____

24 OCTOBER

What you learn is what you die with. – African proverb

Yr_____

_____
_____
_____
_____
_____
_____
_____

Yr_____

_____
_____
_____
_____
_____
_____
_____

Yr_____

_____
_____
_____
_____
_____
_____
_____

25 OCTOBER

By the time the fool has learned the game, the players have dispersed. –
African proverb

Yr_____

_____
_____
_____
_____
_____
_____
_____

Yr_____

_____
_____
_____
_____
_____
_____
_____

Yr_____

_____
_____
_____
_____
_____
_____
_____
_____

26 OCTOBER

Wealth, if you use it, comes to an end; learning, if you use it, increases. –
African proverb

Yr_____

_____

_____

_____

_____

_____

_____

_____

Yr_____

_____

_____

_____

_____

_____

_____

_____

Yr_____

_____

_____

_____

_____

_____

_____

_____

_____

27 OCTOBER

Speak softly and carry a big stick; you will go far. — African proverb

Yr_____

_____
_____
_____
_____
_____
_____
_____
_____

Yr_____

_____
_____
_____
_____
_____
_____
_____

Yr_____

_____
_____
_____
_____
_____
_____
_____
_____

28 OCTOBER

Do not forget what is to be a sailor because of being a captain yourself.
– African proverb

Yr_____

_____
_____
_____
_____
_____
_____
_____
_____

Yr_____

_____
_____
_____
_____
_____
_____
_____
_____

Yr_____

_____
_____
_____
_____
_____
_____
_____
_____

29 OCTOBER

A large chair does not make a king. — African proverb

Yr_____

_____
_____
_____
_____
_____
_____
_____
_____

Yr_____

_____
_____
_____
_____
_____
_____
_____
_____

Yr_____

_____
_____
_____
_____
_____
_____
_____
_____

30 OCTOBER

He who refuses to obey cannot command. – African proverb

Yr_____

_____

_____

_____

_____

_____

_____

_____

Yr_____

_____

_____

_____

_____

_____

_____

_____

Yr_____

_____

_____

_____

_____

_____

_____

_____

_____

31 OCTOBER

A leader who does not take advice is not a leader. – African proverb

Yr____

_____
_____
_____
_____
_____
_____
_____

Yr____

_____
_____
_____
_____
_____
_____
_____

Yr____

_____
_____
_____
_____
_____
_____
_____
_____

1 NOVEMBER

Because he lost his reputation, he lost a kingdom. — African proverb

Yr_____

_____
_____
_____
_____
_____
_____
_____

Yr_____

_____
_____
_____
_____
_____
_____

Yr_____

_____
_____
_____
_____
_____
_____
_____

2 NOVEMBER

If the cockroach wants to rule over the chicken, then it must hire the fox as a body-guard.   — African proverb

Yr_____

_____
_____
_____
_____
_____
_____
_____

Yr_____

_____
_____
_____
_____
_____
_____
_____

Yr_____

_____
_____
_____
_____
_____
_____
_____
_____

3 NOVEMBER

Instruction in youth is like engraving in stone. - African proverb

Yr_____

_____
_____
_____
_____
_____
_____
_____
_____

Yr_____

_____
_____
_____
_____
_____
_____
_____
_____

Yr_____

_____
_____
_____
_____
_____
_____
_____
_____

4 NOVEMBER

Traveling is learning. - African Proverb

Yr_____

_____
_____
_____
_____
_____
_____
_____
_____
_____

Yr_____

_____
_____
_____
_____
_____
_____
_____
_____

Yr_____

_____
_____
_____
_____
_____
_____
_____
_____
_____

5 NOVEMBER

Sticks in a bundle are unbreakable. — African Proverb

Yr_____

_____
_____
_____
_____
_____
_____
_____
_____

Yr_____

_____
_____
_____
_____
_____
_____
_____
_____

Yr_____

_____
_____
_____
_____
_____
_____
_____
_____

6 NOVEMBER

It takes a village to raise a child. — African proverb

Yr_____

_____
_____
_____
_____
_____
_____
_____
_____

Yr_____

_____
_____
_____
_____
_____
_____
_____

Yr_____

_____
_____
_____
_____
_____
_____
_____
_____

7 NOVEMBER

Many hands make light work. — African proverb

Yr_____

_____

_____

_____

_____

_____

_____

_____

Yr_____

_____

_____

_____

_____

_____

_____

_____

Yr_____

_____

_____

_____

_____

_____

_____

_____

_____

8 NOVEMBER

Death is neither friend nor foe but the natural end of all mortals. –
African proverb

Yr_____

_____
_____
_____
_____
_____
_____
_____

Yr_____

_____
_____
_____
_____
_____
_____
_____

Yr_____

_____
_____
_____
_____
_____
_____
_____
_____

9 NOVEMBER

No matter what other honors a man attains in life, his womenfolk: his mother, wife, and daughters, are his crowning glory. – African Proverb

Yr_____

_____

_____

_____

_____

_____

_____

_____

Yr_____

_____

_____

_____

_____

_____

_____

Yr_____

_____

_____

_____

_____

_____

_____

_____

10 NOVEMBER

Every man ought to support his village, community, tribe and nation. —
African proverb

Yr_____

_____
_____
_____
_____
_____
_____
_____

Yr_____

_____
_____
_____
_____
_____
_____
_____

Yr_____

_____
_____
_____
_____
_____
_____
_____
_____

11 NOVEMBER

The child who will not heed the words of his mother, hear the threats of his father, attend to the wisdom of the elders, beckon to the wooing of the priest, must taste the swipe of the rattan. – African proverb

Yr_____

_____

_____

_____

_____

_____

_____

_____

Yr_____

_____

_____

_____

_____

_____

_____

Yr_____

_____

_____

_____

_____

_____

_____

_____

12 NOVEMBER

A man who will not chasten his own child bears the ruin of his family upon his head; for the twig, when you as directed, will grow. – African proverb

Yr____

_____
_____
_____
_____
_____
_____
_____

Yr____

_____
_____
_____
_____
_____
_____
_____

Yr____

_____
_____
_____
_____
_____
_____
_____
_____
_____

13 NOVEMBER

Where there are many, nothing goes wrong. — African proverb

Yr_____

_____

_____

_____

_____

_____

_____

_____

Yr_____

_____

_____

_____

_____

_____

_____

_____

Yr_____

_____

_____

_____

_____

_____

_____

_____

14 NOVEMBER

A single bracelet does not jingle. — African proverb

Yr_____

_____
_____
_____
_____
_____
_____
_____
_____
_____

Yr_____

_____
_____
_____
_____
_____
_____
_____
_____

Yr_____

_____
_____
_____
_____
_____
_____
_____
_____
_____

15 NOVEMBER

A single stick May smoke, but it will not burn. – African proverb

Yr_____

_____

_____

_____

_____

_____

_____

_____

Yr_____

_____

_____

_____

_____

_____

_____

Yr_____

_____

_____

_____

_____

_____

_____

_____

16 NOVEMBER

A family is like a forest, when you are outside it is dense, when you are inside you see that each tree has its place. – African proverb

Yr_____

_____
_____
_____
_____
_____
_____
_____

Yr_____

_____
_____
_____
_____
_____
_____
_____

Yr_____

_____
_____
_____
_____
_____
_____
_____
_____

17 NOVEMBER

By labor comes wealth. — African proverb

Yr_____

_____
_____
_____
_____
_____
_____
_____

Yr_____

_____
_____
_____
_____
_____
_____
_____

Yr_____

_____
_____
_____
_____
_____
_____
_____
_____

18 NOVEMBER

If you watch your pot, your food will not burn. — *African proverb*

Yr_____

_____
_____
_____
_____
_____
_____
_____

Yr_____

_____
_____
_____
_____
_____
_____

Yr_____

_____
_____
_____
_____
_____
_____
_____
_____

19 NOVEMBER

Those who build to themselves shrines and monuments must not neglect to build the true monument of them all...character. – African proverb

Yr_____

_____
_____
_____
_____
_____
_____
_____

Yr_____

_____
_____
_____
_____
_____
_____
_____

Yr_____

_____
_____
_____
_____
_____
_____
_____

20 NOVEMBER

We have two ears and one mouth; which means we ought to listen twice as much as we speak. — African proverb

Yr_____

_____

_____

_____

_____

_____

_____

Yr_____

_____

_____

_____

_____

_____

_____

Yr_____

_____

_____

_____

_____

_____

_____

_____

21 NOVEMBER

He who picks on the weak to display his strength is twice the coward that he is. – African proverb

Yr_____

_____

_____

_____

_____

_____

_____

_____

Yr_____

_____

_____

_____

_____

_____

_____

_____

Yr_____

_____

_____

_____

_____

_____

_____

_____

22 NOVEMBER

A close friend can become a close enemy. – African proverb

Yr_____

_____
_____
_____
_____
_____
_____
_____
_____

Yr_____

_____
_____
_____
_____
_____
_____
_____
_____

Yr_____

_____
_____
_____
_____
_____
_____
_____
_____

23 NOVEMBER

Between true friends even water drunk together is sweet enough. –
African proverb

Yr_____

_____

_____

_____

_____

_____

_____

_____

_____

Yr_____

_____

_____

_____

_____

_____

_____

_____

_____

Yr_____

_____

_____

_____

_____

_____

_____

_____

_____

24 NOVEMBER

What goes around comes around. If you put out good, good finds you and returns to you a hundred-fold. — African proverb

Yr_____

_____
_____
_____
_____
_____
_____
_____

Yr_____

_____
_____
_____
_____
_____
_____
_____

Yr_____

_____
_____
_____
_____
_____
_____
_____

25 NOVEMBER

A small house will hold a hundred friends. – African proverb

Yr_____

_____
_____
_____
_____
_____
_____
_____
_____

Yr_____

_____
_____
_____
_____
_____
_____
_____

Yr_____

_____
_____
_____
_____
_____
_____
_____
_____

26 NOVEMBER

Beware of the flattering tongue. It swings its talon in the wild delirium and sweeps the simple off their feet. – African proverb

Yr_____

_____
_____
_____
_____
_____
_____
_____

Yr_____

_____
_____
_____
_____
_____
_____
_____

Yr_____

_____
_____
_____
_____
_____
_____
_____

27 NOVEMBER

It is no shame at all to work for money. — African proverb

Yr____

_____

_____

_____

_____

_____

_____

_____

Yr____

_____

_____

_____

_____

_____

_____

Yr____

_____

_____

_____

_____

_____

_____

_____

28 NOVEMBER

Show me your friend and I will show you your character. — African proverb

Yr_____

_____

_____

_____

_____

_____

_____

_____

Yr_____

_____

_____

_____

_____

_____

_____

_____

Yr_____

_____

_____

_____

_____

_____

_____

_____

29 NOVEMBER

One cannot count on riches. – African proverb

Yr_____

_____
_____
_____
_____
_____
_____
_____

Yr_____

_____
_____
_____
_____
_____
_____
_____

Yr_____

_____
_____
_____
_____
_____
_____
_____
_____

30 NOVEMBER

He who wants what another has has ambition. Let him carve out his own success. – African proverb

Yr_____

_____
_____
_____
_____
_____
_____
_____

Yr_____

_____
_____
_____
_____
_____
_____
_____

Yr_____

_____
_____
_____
_____
_____
_____
_____
_____

1 DECEMBER

Children are the reward of life. – African proverb

Yr_____

_____

_____

_____

_____

_____

_____

_____

Yr_____

_____

_____

_____

_____

_____

_____

_____

Yr_____

_____

_____

_____

_____

_____

_____

_____

_____

2 DECEMBER

The old woman looks after the child to grow its teeth and the young one in turn looks after the old woman when she loses her teeth. — African proverb

Yr_____

_____

_____

_____

_____

_____

_____

_____

Yr_____

_____

_____

_____

_____

_____

_____

_____

Yr_____

_____

_____

_____

_____

_____

_____

_____

_____

3 DECEMBER

He who earns calamity, eats it with his family. - African proverb

Yr_____

_____

_____

_____

_____

_____

_____

_____

Yr_____

_____

_____

_____

_____

_____

_____

_____

Yr_____

_____

_____

_____

_____

_____

_____

_____

_____

4 DECEMBER

Poverty is slavery. - African Proverb

Yr_____

_____
_____
_____
_____
_____
_____
_____

Yr_____

_____
_____
_____
_____
_____
_____
_____

Yr_____

_____
_____
_____
_____
_____
_____
_____

5 DECEMBER

When you rush into the world, the world rushes back at you. – African Proverb

Yr_____

_____
_____
_____
_____
_____
_____
_____

Yr_____

_____
_____
_____
_____
_____
_____
_____

Yr_____

_____
_____
_____
_____
_____
_____
_____

6 DECEMBER

Neglecting a tiny sore could cost you a leg. — African proverb

Yr_____

_____
_____
_____
_____
_____
_____
_____

Yr_____

_____
_____
_____
_____
_____
_____
_____

Yr_____

_____
_____
_____
_____
_____
_____
_____
_____

7 DECEMBER

Bad friends will prevent you from having good friends. — African proverb

Yr_____

_____

_____

_____

_____

_____

_____

_____

Yr_____

_____

_____

_____

_____

_____

_____

_____

Yr_____

_____

_____

_____

_____

_____

_____

_____

8 DECEMBER

You can never sneak dawn past a healthy rooster. – African proverb

Yr_____

_____
_____
_____
_____
_____
_____
_____
_____

Yr_____

_____
_____
_____
_____
_____
_____
_____
_____

Yr_____

_____
_____
_____
_____
_____
_____
_____
_____

9 DECEMBER

Oil and water will never mix. One will sink to the bottom and the other will float on top. – African Proverb

Yr_____

_____
_____
_____
_____
_____
_____
_____

Yr_____

_____
_____
_____
_____
_____
_____
_____

Yr_____

_____
_____
_____
_____
_____
_____
_____
_____

10 DECEMBER

Money can't talk, yet it can make lies look true. — African proverb

Yr_____

_____
_____
_____
_____
_____
_____
_____

Yr_____

_____
_____
_____
_____
_____
_____
_____

Yr_____

_____
_____
_____
_____
_____
_____
_____

11 DECEMBER

The skin of the leopard is beautiful, but not his heart. – African proverb

Yr_____

_____
_____
_____
_____
_____
_____
_____

Yr_____

_____
_____
_____
_____
_____
_____
_____

Yr_____

_____
_____
_____
_____
_____
_____
_____

12 DECEMBER

The surface of the water is beautiful, but it is no good to sleep on. –
African proverb

Yr_____

_____
_____
_____
_____
_____
_____
_____

Yr_____

_____
_____
_____
_____
_____
_____
_____

Yr_____

_____
_____
_____
_____
_____
_____
_____

13 DECEMBER

Judge not your beauty by the number of people who look at you, but rather by the number of people who smile at you. – African proverb

Yr_____

_____
_____
_____
_____
_____
_____
_____

Yr_____

_____
_____
_____
_____
_____
_____
_____

Yr_____

_____
_____
_____
_____
_____
_____
_____

14 DECEMBER

He who loves the vase loves also what is inside. — African proverb

Yr_____

_____
_____
_____
_____
_____
_____
_____

Yr_____

_____
_____
_____
_____
_____
_____
_____

Yr_____

_____
_____
_____
_____
_____
_____
_____

15 DECEMBER

Coffee and love taste best when hot. – African proverb

Yr_____

_____
_____
_____
_____
_____
_____
_____

Yr_____

_____
_____
_____
_____
_____
_____
_____

Yr_____

_____
_____
_____
_____
_____
_____
_____
_____

16 DECEMBER

If you marry a monkey for its wealth, the money goes and the monkey remains as is. — African proverb

Yr_____

_____
_____
_____
_____
_____
_____
_____

Yr_____

_____
_____
_____
_____
_____
_____

Yr_____

_____
_____
_____
_____
_____
_____
_____
_____

17 DECEMBER

Love has to be shown by deeds not words. – African proverb

Yr_____

_____
_____
_____
_____
_____
_____
_____

Yr_____

_____
_____
_____
_____
_____
_____
_____

Yr_____

_____
_____
_____
_____
_____
_____
_____

18 DECEMBER

Always being in a hurry does not prevent death, neither does going slowly prevent living. — African proverb

Yr_____

_____
_____
_____
_____
_____
_____
_____

Yr_____

_____
_____
_____
_____
_____
_____
_____

Yr_____

_____
_____
_____
_____
_____
_____
_____

19 DECEMBER

The man who counts the bits of food he swallows is never satisfied. –
African proverb

Yr_____

_____

_____

_____

_____

_____

_____

_____

Yr_____

_____

_____

_____

_____

_____

_____

_____

Yr_____

_____

_____

_____

_____

_____

_____

_____

20 DECEMBER

Food gained by fraud tastes sweet to a man, but he ends up with gravel in his mouth. – African proverb

Yr_____

_____
_____
_____
_____
_____
_____
_____

Yr_____

_____
_____
_____
_____
_____
_____
_____

Yr_____

_____
_____
_____
_____
_____
_____
_____
_____

21 DECEMBER

A spider's cobweb isn't only its sleeping spring but also its food trap. –
African proverb

Yr_____

_____
_____
_____
_____
_____
_____
_____

Yr_____

_____
_____
_____
_____
_____
_____

Yr_____

_____
_____
_____
_____
_____
_____
_____

22 DECEMBER

Happiness is as good as food. — African proverb

Yr_____

_____
_____
_____
_____
_____
_____
_____
_____

Yr_____

_____
_____
_____
_____
_____
_____
_____

Yr_____

_____
_____
_____
_____
_____
_____
_____
_____

23 DECEMBER

If I am in harmony with my family, that's success. — African proverb

Yr_____

_____
_____
_____
_____
_____
_____
_____
_____

Yr_____

_____
_____
_____
_____
_____
_____
_____

Yr_____

_____
_____
_____
_____
_____
_____
_____
_____

24 DECEMBER

If relatives help each other, what evil can hurt them? – African proverb

Yr_____

_____
_____
_____
_____
_____
_____
_____
_____

Yr_____

_____
_____
_____
_____
_____
_____
_____
_____

Yr_____

_____
_____
_____
_____
_____
_____
_____
_____
_____

25 DECEMBER

True celebration is shared, not savored in isolation by oneself alone. –
African proverb

Yr_____

_____
_____
_____
_____
_____
_____
_____
_____

Yr_____

_____
_____
_____
_____
_____
_____
_____

Yr_____

_____
_____
_____
_____
_____
_____
_____
_____

26 DECEMBER

You cannot sew together a leaf once torn apart. – African proverb

Yr_____

_____
_____
_____
_____
_____
_____
_____
_____

Yr_____

_____
_____
_____
_____
_____
_____
_____

Yr_____

_____
_____
_____
_____
_____
_____
_____
_____

27 DECEMBER

The friends of our friends are our friends. – African proverb

Yr_____

_____

_____

_____

_____

_____

_____

_____

_____

Yr_____

_____

_____

_____

_____

_____

_____

_____

Yr_____

_____

_____

_____

_____

_____

_____

_____

_____

28 DECEMBER

You should not hoard your money and die of hunger. – African proverb

Yr_____

_____

_____

_____

_____

_____

_____

_____

_____

Yr_____

_____

_____

_____

_____

_____

_____

_____

_____

Yr_____

_____

_____

_____

_____

_____

_____

_____

_____

29 DECEMBER

You can never put back into its shell an egg which has been cracked open. – African proverb

Yr_____

_____
_____
_____
_____
_____
_____
_____
_____

Yr_____

_____
_____
_____
_____
_____
_____
_____

Yr_____

_____
_____
_____
_____
_____
_____
_____
_____

30 DECEMBER

The most beautiful fig May contain a worm. — African proverb

Yr_____

_____
_____
_____
_____
_____
_____
_____
_____

Yr_____

_____
_____
_____
_____
_____
_____
_____

Yr_____

_____
_____
_____
_____
_____
_____
_____
_____

31 DECEMBER

Wisdom does not just simply flow from the lips of even the wise; it must be coaxed, cajoled and nursed before it will come forth...even then haltingly. – African proverb

Yr_____

_____
_____
_____
_____
_____
_____
_____
_____

Yr_____

_____
_____
_____
_____
_____
_____
_____

Yr_____

_____
_____
_____
_____
_____
_____
_____
_____

www.ingramcontent.com/pod-product-compliance
Lightning Source LLC
Chambersburg PA
CBHW060325100426
42812CB00003B/882